# REAL ESTATE CAREERS

*A Career Concise Guide*

# REAL ESTATE CAREERS

### by Jim Haskins

**PHOTOGRAPHS BY CHUCK FREEDMAN**
**FRANKLIN WATTS**
**NEW YORK | LONDON | 1978**

ST. PHILIPS COLLEGE LIBRARY

Acknowledgments

For their cooperation in producing the photos for this book, the photographer would like to thank Pat Button and George Lawrence of Lawrence Management, Elliot Greene of Helmsley-Spear, Henry Schwier, and Steve Levens.

Library of Congress Cataloging in Publication Data

Haskins, James, 1941–
    Real estate careers.

    (A Career concise guide)
    Bibliography: p.
    Includes index.
    SUMMARY: Describes the educational requirements and opportunities for a variety of careers in the real estate industry.
    1. Real estate business—Vocational guidance—Juvenile literature. [1. Real estate business—Vocational guidance. 2. Vocational guidance] I. Freedman, Chuck. II. Title.
HD1375.H39      333.3′3      77-15647
ISBN 0-531-01423-1

Copyright © 1978 by Franklin Watts, Inc.
All rights reserved
Printed in the United States of America
5 4 3 2

# Contents

Introduction
**1**

Brokerage
**4**
Sales
**20**
Management
**34**
Appraisal
**45**
Investment
**49**
Government Service
**52**
Publications
**57**
Ethics
**57**

For Further Information
**61**
For Further Reading
**63**
Index
**64**

FOR SALE
Realty USA
GREENWICH
692-7616
FOR SALE
MLS
CLINE
SARATOGA
584-2800

# Introduction

What is real estate? First and foremost, it is the land. But of course real estate is not only the land, but also an extraordinary number of things that are permanently a part of it. There is the air space above, the minerals, oil, and gas below it, and of course the buildings standing on its surface.

Today the real estate industry is one of the biggest in North America. Houses, apartment buildings, shopping centers, office buildings, warehouses, hotels, motels, industrial buildings, and above all the land itself are constantly being bought and sold.

Ours is a highly mobile society. A hundred years ago a family might expect to settle in a small town and remain there for the rest of their lives. Their children would grow up, marry, and stay in the same town to raise the next generation. But today families are constantly on the move. Skilled workers often move to find work in their specialized field. Executives working for large corporations are shuttled from one plant or office to another to broaden their work experience. Businesses outgrow their offices or plants and move to bigger ones, or ones more suited to their needs.

Every time a family moves, an office expands, a store moves to a different location, or a plant looks for a new facility better suited to its needs, a real estate professional is involved, whether as a broker, a salesperson, a property manager, or an appraiser. And when you realize that between 1965 and 1974, 41.8 percent of the population moved, you can see that the real estate industry touches upon an enormous number of people at some time in their lives. Everyone has to live somewhere, whether in an apartment, a house, a condominium, a cooperative, or a mobile home. Everyone has to work somewhere, whether it is in an office, a plant, a store, a restaurant, a hotel, or a motel. Even a truck driver, who certainly doesn't work *in* an office, will still be dropping by the company's office to get information about his or her next job.

Want to go to a museum or an art gallery on a rainy day? Real estate will keep the rain off while you improve your mind. Want to get a book for entertainment reading, or do you need to do research for a term paper? Then there's the library—real estate again. Bowling alleys, basketball courts, tennis courts—there is no end to it.

And if real estate seems to be a mammoth collection of inanimate objects, then you must understand before you read further that careers in real estate touch upon far more than dollars and cents. Real estate would not exist in many cases if people did not need it for one purpose or another. What makes real estate an exciting area to work in is the fact that it is about *people.* Real estate professionals address themselves primarily to the needs of human beings.

For instance, it is not in the interests of a property manager to pressure someone into signing a lease for office premises that aren't *quite* what the person is looking for. It definitely is not good business for a super salesperson to hurry the Smiths into buying a house more expensive than they can comfortably afford. Of course, nothing and no one is perfect in this world, and people do get sucked in by fast-talking brokers and salespeople and end up suffering financial loss or personal inconvenience as a result. But the real estate professional organizations are constantly alert, keeping a watchful eye on their membership.

When the average person thinks about real estate,

he or she thinks in terms of the real estate broker, but there are other areas of real estate that provide important and interesting careers.

However, there is one personal characteristic all real estate people share, and it is an important one to consider when you are thinking about a career in the industry. Anyone who is involved in the real estate business must be able to deal every day with the fact that they are handling a commodity whose value is constantly changing. There are no absolute values that can be fixed for even a year at a time. There are only *estimates* of value, and they can change very rapidly indeed. When the economy is booming, so is the real estate industry. Buildings are constructed, homes are built. But when the economy slumps, so does real estate. New construction slows down or stops altogether. People are less mobile, preferring to stay put until things improve.

Then there are the local, state, and federal laws affecting every kind of real estate, laws that are constantly changing. A real estate professional cannot rely on guesswork, the "I think it was okay last year" attitude. Zoning laws change, building codes change. Neighborhoods deteriorate, and the question arises, how far will they go? Will they go all the way down to the slum level, leading to abandonment by owners and consequent tax losses to the community? Or will they stop at medium-shabby and slowly improve again? The real estate professional must be in touch with such trends, whatever they are.

Real estate lies at the heart of human existence, affecting how we live, work, play, and go to school. The real estate professional must be a community person, someone to whom work is a seven-day-a-week concern. The real estate industry is not the right place for the nine-to-fiver who wants to forget all about work at the end of the day.

# Brokerage

## WHAT IS A BROKER?

A real estate broker is an agent, a representative. He or she is generally hired by the owner of a property either to negotiate the sale to a buyer or to lease the property to a tenant. Brokerages are small businesses that employ salespeople to do the selling, while the broker acquires the right to sell (or lease).

Sometimes the broker acts for both buyer and seller as a "middle man," but this is only legal if both parties approve. A broker who represents both parties without telling them what is going on is being unethical, and can (and indeed should) lose his or her license.

All states now require by law that a real estate broker have a license before going into business. When the newly licensed broker opens an office, that license must be prominently displayed on the wall for all to see. THE NATIONAL ASSOCIATION OF REALTORS® has been working hard for a number of years to upgrade the standards of education and professional conduct among brokers and other real estate people. Real estate is a respectable profession, where high standards of conduct are demanded.

So, what kind of person becomes a real estate broker?

John S. is typical of many young people going into brokerage in the seventies. He attended a two-year college where he took courses in business management, economics, and real estate practice. After he obtained his real estate salesperson's license, he went to work for a broker in the suburban area of the midwestern city where he grew up.

"I'd had a couple of years' experience as a clerk with an insurance company, and I won't say that it was time wasted. But I knew I didn't want to do it for the rest of my life," he says. "And then I got a job in a real estate office, handling paperwork, taking phone messages for the salespeople, and generally making myself useful. And after two years of that, when I was twenty-five, I went to the owner and asked to be considered for a job as a junior salesperson. I knew the junior salesperson was leaving. We had a long talk, and we really went into the details. I knew, and had known for a couple of years, that I would be expected to support myself for the first six months until commissions started coming in. I had achieved my savings goal.

"I was lucky. The broker and the senior salesperson I worked with were both very experienced, and I got excellent training on the job. And then, after I'd been promoted to senior salesperson and had done that successfully for a couple of years, my wife and I were left a little money by a relative. It was the combination of my experience and the backing of a little capital to tide us over that convinced me to go into business as a broker."

John had been a broker for about a year when we talked to him, so the problems of running a small business were still very fresh in his mind.

"One of the first things you learn," John said, "is that nothing remains the same for any length of time in the real estate business. It doesn't matter whether you're selling or you're a broker. You are going to be dealing every single day of your life with something which is constantly changing. The unexpected is our daily business. You can study the books until you're blue in the face, and believe me you *must* have that theoretical background in your head. But the learning process has only just begun when you get your license. You think you know a lot, but you don't! If you're a broker, the education is a continuing thing. It never stops.

"You're studying changing property values *all* day, *all* week, *all* year. You're studying changing neighborhoods, changing federal and state laws, zoning. Is there a highway program in the works? If so, where is it going to hit in your area? Even if it goes through a more distant area of town, it is still going to affect property values in *your* part of town. The local newspapers, the national press, the trade publications, the new books on real estate which come out every year, courses on allied subjects—somehow I manage it all. Being in real estate is settling for a lifetime's study of literally dozens of subjects. I love it!"

When John set up his own business, the first thing he had to deal with was his position as an employer. He knew that he was strong on selling, but he had less practical experience of administration than his wife.

Anne S. says, "We talked about it for a long time before John actually made the great move. We'd always had it in mind, and he had wanted that sales experience before he tackled the business of being a broker. We had come across so many people starting up small businesses of one kind or another, so we had *heard* of some of the pitfalls at least. John is a terrific salesman. He knows his product, and his overly orderly work habits were a plus for someone starting up on his own. We both knew that I loved the nitty gritty stuff of running a business. I had taken courses in bookkeeping over the years, and before we took the plunge I had taken some accounting courses to beef up my knowledge. And most important of all, we both took courses in business administration. Oh, we'd had friends who'd gone bust because they'd over-expanded too fast, the economy had slumped, and they were caught in the middle."

John joined in: "We *planned.* That legacy I mentioned enabled us to go ahead a year or two sooner than we'd expected to. But the point is, we didn't wake up one morning and say to each other, 'Hey, let's open a brokerage, it's a nice sunny day!'"

"No, that's right," Anne laughed. "But you'd be surprised the number of people who plunge ahead without doing any planning at all. There is this idea people have that they want to be 'their own masters,' 'to be free.' Well, actually you have much more freedom as an employee, because you can always say, 'Well, I can't solve this problem, I'm going home.' If it's your business, you've got to stay and solve that problem. About the only freedom you have in running your own business is the freedom to make your own mistakes, without having someone climbing all over you afterwards. When you're an employee, you can always come up with an alibi. But an alibi isn't going to help at all when you're the boss."

"We'd had a steady savings program over the years," John went on, "and Anne's having a job was an incredible help in building capital. We decided to start off with three salesmen, and we decided that Anne would handle the office end of things in a practical day-to-day sense."

"One of the first problems when you start a small business," Anne said, "is hiring personnel. Now, everyone *thinks* they know who they want and who they don't. But when you're faced with a person on the other side of the desk, and you have to find out a great deal of detailed information about them, well, let's say it takes thought! John and I had studied books on the subject, so I worked out a formula once and for all with a long series of questions and a detailed method of rating the interviewees. Frankly, we were plain lucky. You can go through all the right steps and still be wrong about someone. But our three salespeople are hard workers, steady workers, and most important of all, they know *how* to work. They are much the same kind of salespeople that John was; they set reasonable goals for themselves and meet them. They plan each day, each week, each month."

"We hold weekly and monthly meetings," John went on. "I discuss their work with them constantly. I discuss the business with them, so they feel they're not just out there chasing commissions but are a part of the business. Because of my experience as a salesperson, I know what they should be doing in terms of business. So, I am not like a certain broker I know who sets goals which are unrealistic for his salespeople. He's having a very high turnover, because his goals are impossible. It isn't that you are going to be easy on your salespeople, just realistic in what you expect of them."

We asked John about the change from being an employee to being the boss.

"I was determined not to compete with my salespeople," he said. "This is one of the most common faults with a nervous new broker, especially if he has a background as a salesperson. No, I regard myself as a supervisor, and one of the first rules for a good supervisor is to delegate responsibility. I regard myself as a general contact man around town. I don't know how many people I talk to every year, people in city and state government, architects in business for themselves, architects employed by the government, engineers, other real estate people; the list is endless. And because my wife and I have roots in the community—I coach the Little League team, she's active with the Girl Scouts and does volunteer work with underprivileged children, and of course we're both busy in church affairs—Anne and I both know an enormous number of people living and working in the area where *we* are living and doing business."

**A broker spends a lot of time telephoning and checking property lists.**

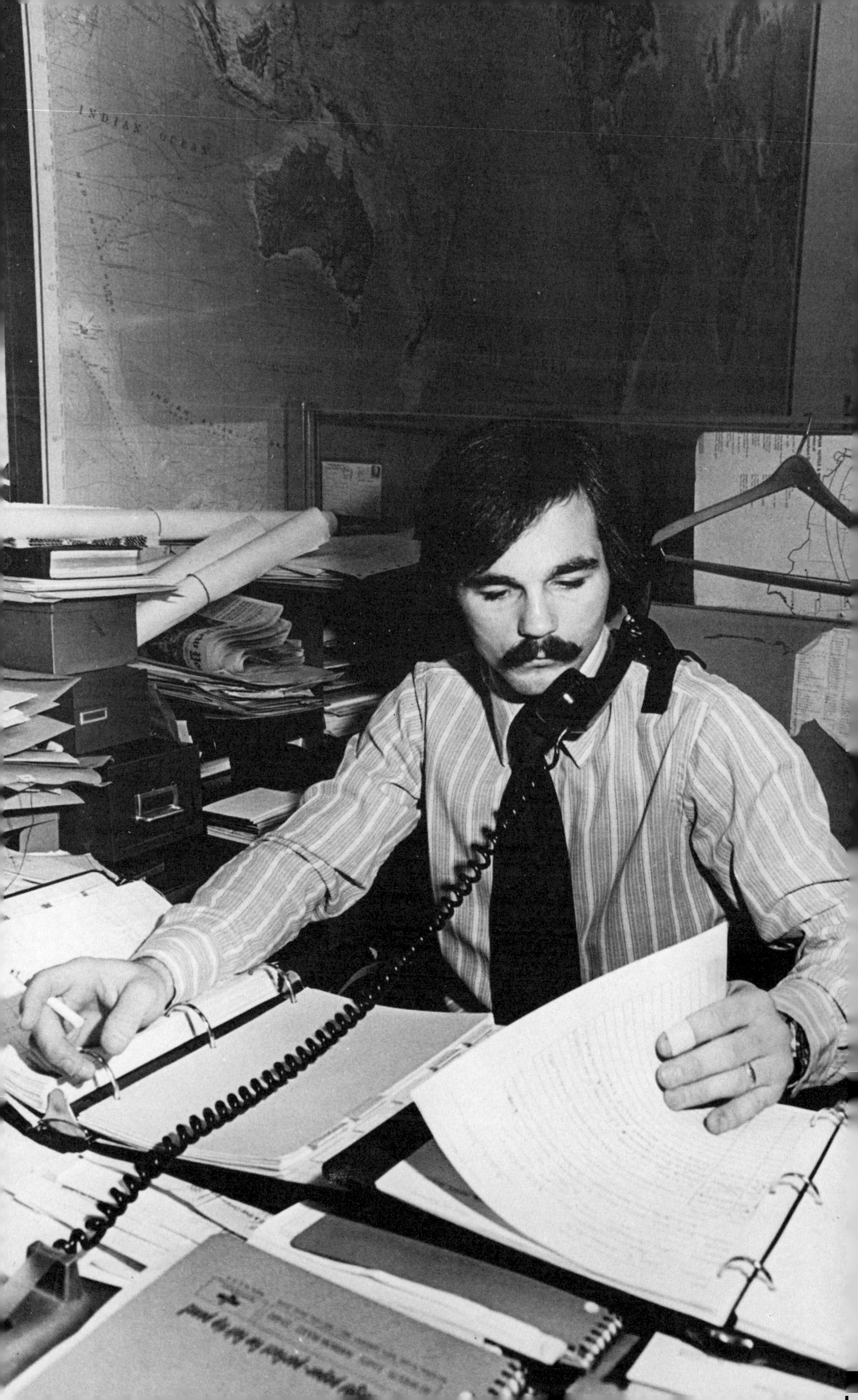
INDIAN OCEAN

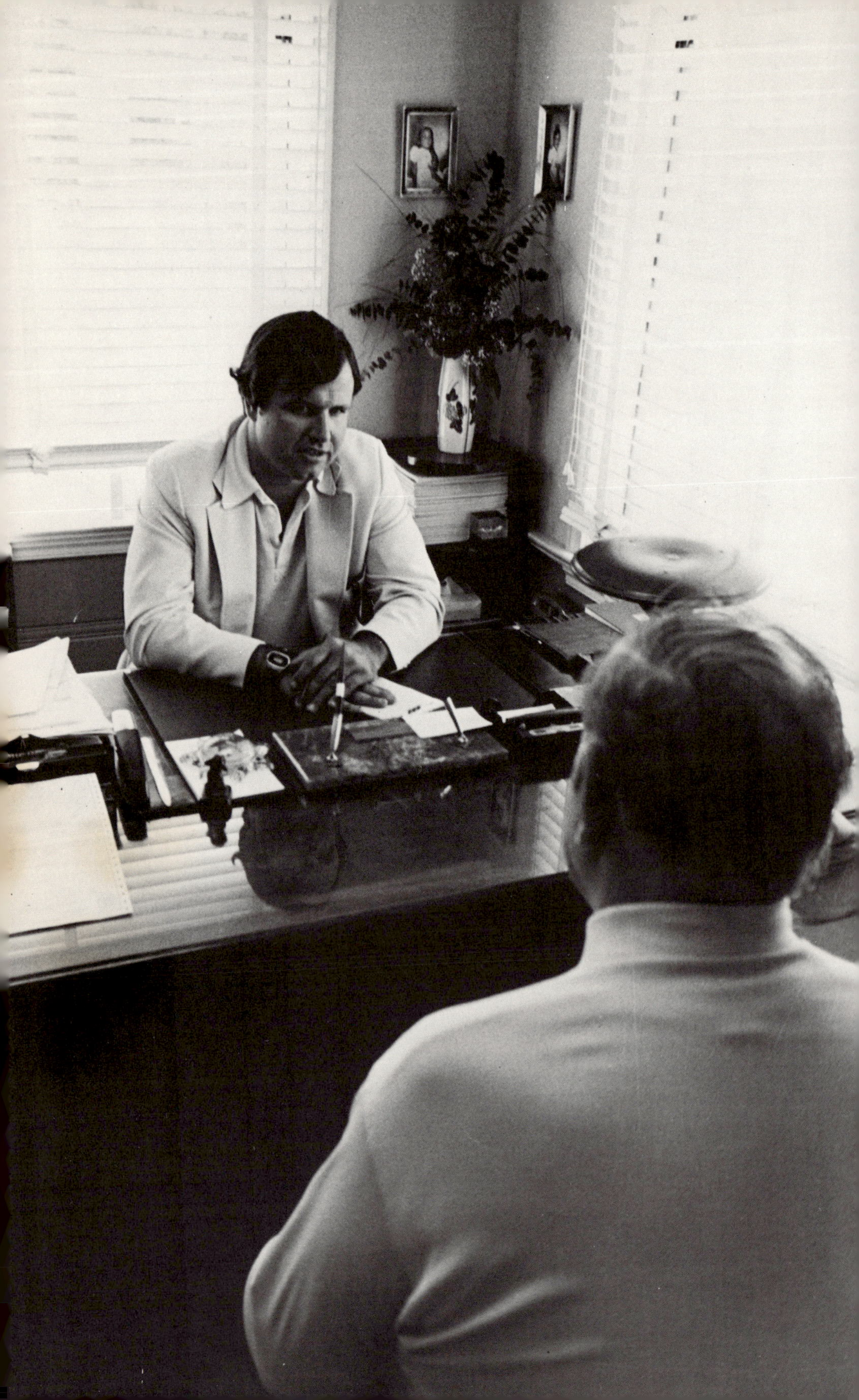

"One of the major changes in the past ten years is that a couple of big corporations have moved their headquarters to our town, and that has meant a lot more turnover in the community. Executives are transferred here for a year or two. They buy houses, settle in, and then the company moves them on again to another part of the country. There is great turnover in real estate in the residential section. I'm constantly in touch with the personnel people in the company. When one corporation moves into town, others are likely to follow. There has been an increase in office construction in the downtown area, and this in turn can mean more people buying homes in the suburbs. Those engineers, architects, employees of city and state government often become good friends over the years. Their kids go to school with my kids. We're all active in the community. We live here. It isn't just dollars and cents—it's our home, our kids' home. I have more than a financial interest in the community; I have a personal commitment to it."

## COMMERCIAL BROKER

Joel F. is in his early thirties. He opened his own brokerage office in northern California two years ago. His background was as a salesperson specializing in commercial properties—retail stores, office buildings, and so on.

He says, "When I first got out of the marines I joined a brokerage firm which specialized in leasing of commercial properties, because to me office buildings are the exciting thing in selling real estate. There's the diversity—no two days are the same. Take yesterday. I

**A commercial broker with a client who is interested in buying a motel.**

talked to two women in the morning who had decided to open a beauty shop. They were both experienced as managers of beauty shops, so they knew what they were getting into. We discussed location and the kind of clientele they wanted to attract. When someone is opening a store that depends on the merchandise in the window to bring in customers from the street, and it's in an area of the country that gets very hot in summer, then they're going to want a store on the shady side of the street. Sun fades merchandise in the window, and anyway, people pick the shady side to walk along. But for a beauty shop it isn't so important. Most of their customers call for an appointment at a specific time. The shop doesn't rely on casual drop-in trade to any extent. So even if they're on the sunny side of the street, they can have shades in the windows to keep the heat out.

"But for a beauty shop it's important that they don't find themselves with a competitor two doors away. And this is where a broker is essential, because it is my business to keep the different kinds of stores in the downtown area in my head. They'd seen a for-rent sign on a store which seemed ideal to them, but I was able to steer them to another location because I'd heard on the real estate grapevine that another beauty shop was about to open across the street."

Joel employs a secretary and two salesmen, and he sells as well as being the boss and general contact man. He is in an area with increasing commercial development, and his office is on Main Street, right in the heart of the properties for which he negotiates sales and leases.

## LAND BROKER

This is yet another specialty. For example, if a doctor, lawyer, or other professional wants to buy agricultural land as an investment and protect his or her money from high taxes, a land broker will be involved. Sometimes people buy land with the intention of building on it later—a vacation home or perhaps a house that they intend to rent for income purposes.

But whatever the reason for purchase, a broker specializing in land must know all about the zoning for the particular area. Suppose someone buys a farm as an investment, and the broker doesn't know that a major highway is planned within five years that will cut straight through the middle. The buyer is going to lose money, perhaps a great deal of money. Similarly, if a couple buys land with the intention of building a vacation home, they have to know certain things about it. Is the soil suitable for the disposal of sewage? What about water lines? What about access roads? Suppose a couple, both artists, buy a piece of land on which to build not only a house but a studio to work in. The broker must be able to tell them whether it is legal for them to build a studio in that particular area, which is residential. Zoning laws vary a good deal, and the studio might or might not be considered a commercial property.

You can see how important it is not only to have brokers but to have alert, well-educated brokers who really know their subject.

**INDUSTRIAL BROKER**

Harry M. is an industrial broker whose business lies in selling or renting factories, warehouses, and manufacturing facilities.

We asked Harry what some of the problems are.

"A factory is generally tailor-made for a manufacturer, and when that manufacturer moves out to a new facility, it is sometimes a problem finding a buyer who is really happy with the building. Very often extensive alterations have to be made, so from the broker's point of view the trick is to know enough about the needs of manufacturers in the area to be able to go to them and say, 'Hey, do you need an additional plant? I heard you did. Well, there's this factory that so-and-so is moving out of next month. Let me show it to you.' Sometimes you're right, and you have a happy client. Sometimes, you have overlooked some small detail that makes the factory useless to the company you're trying to sell it to. Then, of course, there is the pollution problem. You have to be able to tell a guy what he can and can't do with waste materials. Is the factory in a good location for him to ship in raw materials and ship out the finished product? What may be a good location for one manufacturer may not be suitable for another."

Most brokers do their main business within a three- to five-mile radius of their offices, so a residential broker is going to open an office as close as possible to the residential area where he or she hopes to do business. But the office must still be located in an area of heavy traffic in order to get the drop-in trade. Commercial brokers do not open offices near residential areas. Instead, they look for a location in the heart of the commercial district, somewhere, for example, where the owner of a business who is looking for new offices can see the sign and stop in at lunchtime to discuss potential needs. An industrial broker is going to be located further out of town, nearer to the industrial properties, factories, warehouses, and so on.

If you want to be a real estate broker, you want to be the owner of a small business, and that means being a diplomat, a hard-headed businessperson, knowing your town, knowing your real estate law, being *truly* on top of things.

Being the owner of a small business means more than

being a salesperson. It means being a good administrator, a good hirer of people, a good boss.

You will be setting sales goals for your salespeople to meet, and you will find that not all of them are going to be successful all of the time. You have got to be able to sit down with a man or woman, and, without anger or accusations, try to find out what's wrong. You have got to know what their problems on the job are. And the only way to find that out is to have had experience as a salesperson yourself.

The general feeling is that brokerage firms are more efficiently run than they used to be. A multiple-listing system has been responsible to some extent, since it introduces an element of competition between brokers.

What is a multiple-listing system? An area's local realty board gathers together all sorts of information on properties in the area. The information is recorded and put into a listing. This listing, often including hundreds of properties, is then circulated to all the members of the multiple-listing system. Thus, if you are selling your own house, you are not only going to have prospective buyers from your own broker, but buyers from all the brokers in the area. You the seller have a much wider market, and the brokers and their salespeople are encouraged to work very hard to sell the property. The sale, and therefore the commission (a small, predetermined percentage of the sale price), goes to the first brokerage to sell the property.

It has been established that successful brokerage firms are successful either because the owner has a sound business background and knows exactly what he or she is doing, or because the owner recognizes that he or she knows little or nothing about business, and hires someone with managerial skills to take care of that side of things.

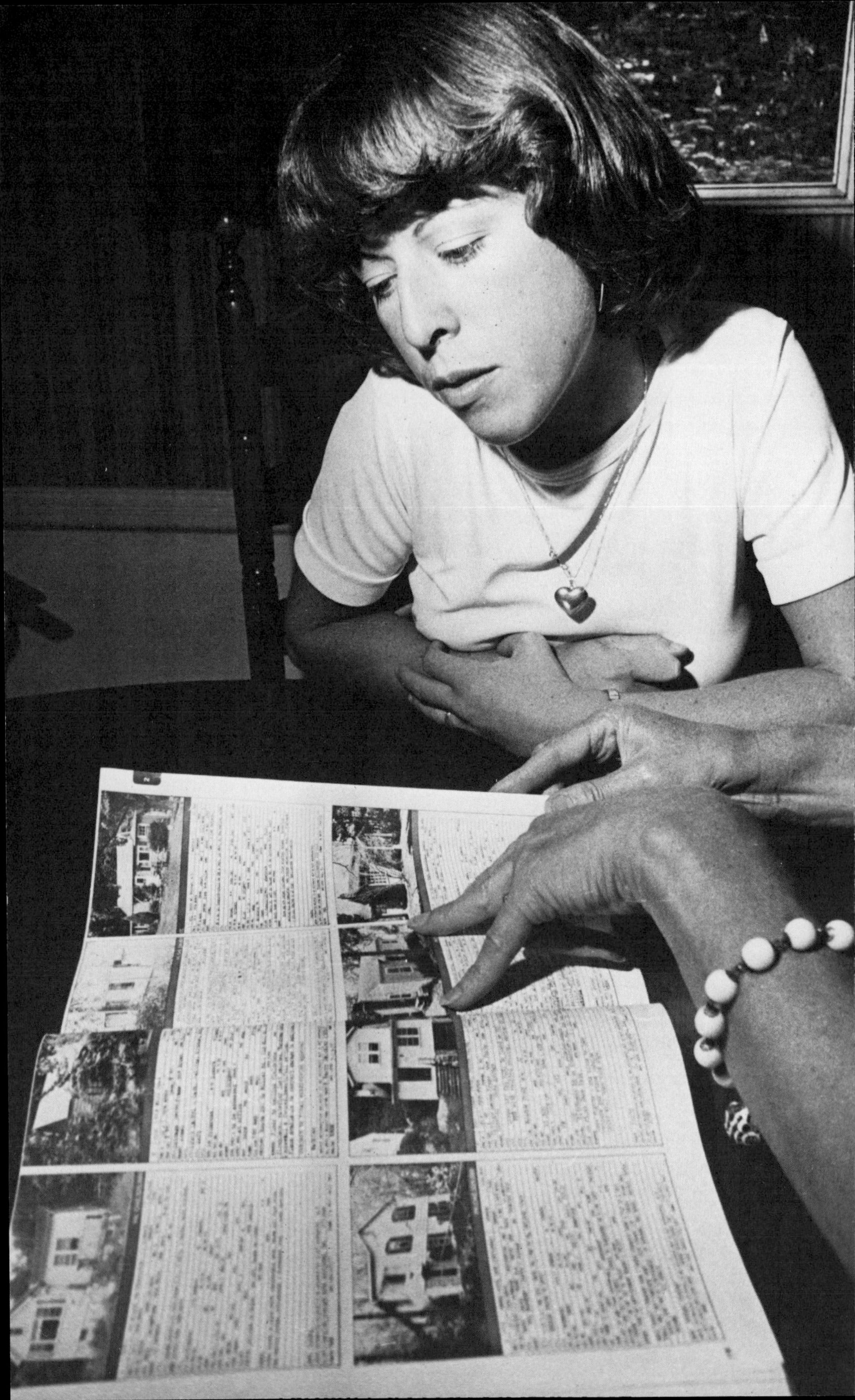

Failures are generally due to one of three basic reasons:
1. Bad sales management and a poor understanding of the market.
2. Bad financial planning.
3. Bad record-keeping, so that no one knew how bad things were until bankruptcy struck.

**EDUCATION**

Many highly successful real estate people are high school graduates, but with the real estate industry becoming more complex every year, college degrees are becoming increasingly necessary. There are now over five hundred universities, colleges, and community colleges offering one or more courses in real estate. That includes some one hundred fifty that offer real estate as a major. Economics, law, banking, finance, architecture, selling, psychology, and business administration are also recommended as useful majors in a career as a broker.

Many state universities offer correspondence courses in real estate, and the YMCA also offers evening courses. The National Association of Realtors, whose address is given in the section "For Further Information," has free booklets available on careers in real estate, a list of universities and colleges offering one or more courses in real estate as a major field, a list of those offering graduate work, and a list of those state universities offering correspondence courses. They will also send you a list of the names and addresses of real estate licensing officials in each state.

**This sales trainee is being shown how to use a multiple-listing book.**

Since licensing requirements differ slightly from state to state, you should be sure of where you want to live and work before you start studying for your licensing exam.

A majority of states require candidates for a broker's license to have a specified amount of experience in selling real estate, or the equivalent in related experience or education (generally one to three years). State licenses are renewed annually without reexamination.

Many real estate boards that are members of the NATIONAL ASSOCIATION OF REALTORS® sponsor courses covering the fundamentals and legal aspects of real estate. And you should check with your local board regarding educational programs they sponsor and regarding career prospects in the area. The Canadian Real Estate Association, whose address can also be found in "For Further Information," will give you educational and career information for Canada.

As a high school graduate, it is possible to get a number of entry-level jobs in the real estate industry. For example you could start out as a file clerk or an office assistant and then hope to progress to rental agent, salesperson, and finally to broker. Salaries for entry-level jobs would be around $150 to $200 a week and could be expected to increase as you gained experience.

**COMMISSIONS**

Commissions (percentage of the sale price, which is the fee paid to the broker on completion of a sale) average

*This clerical worker is learning more about the real estate business; she is thinking about training for a career in real estate.*

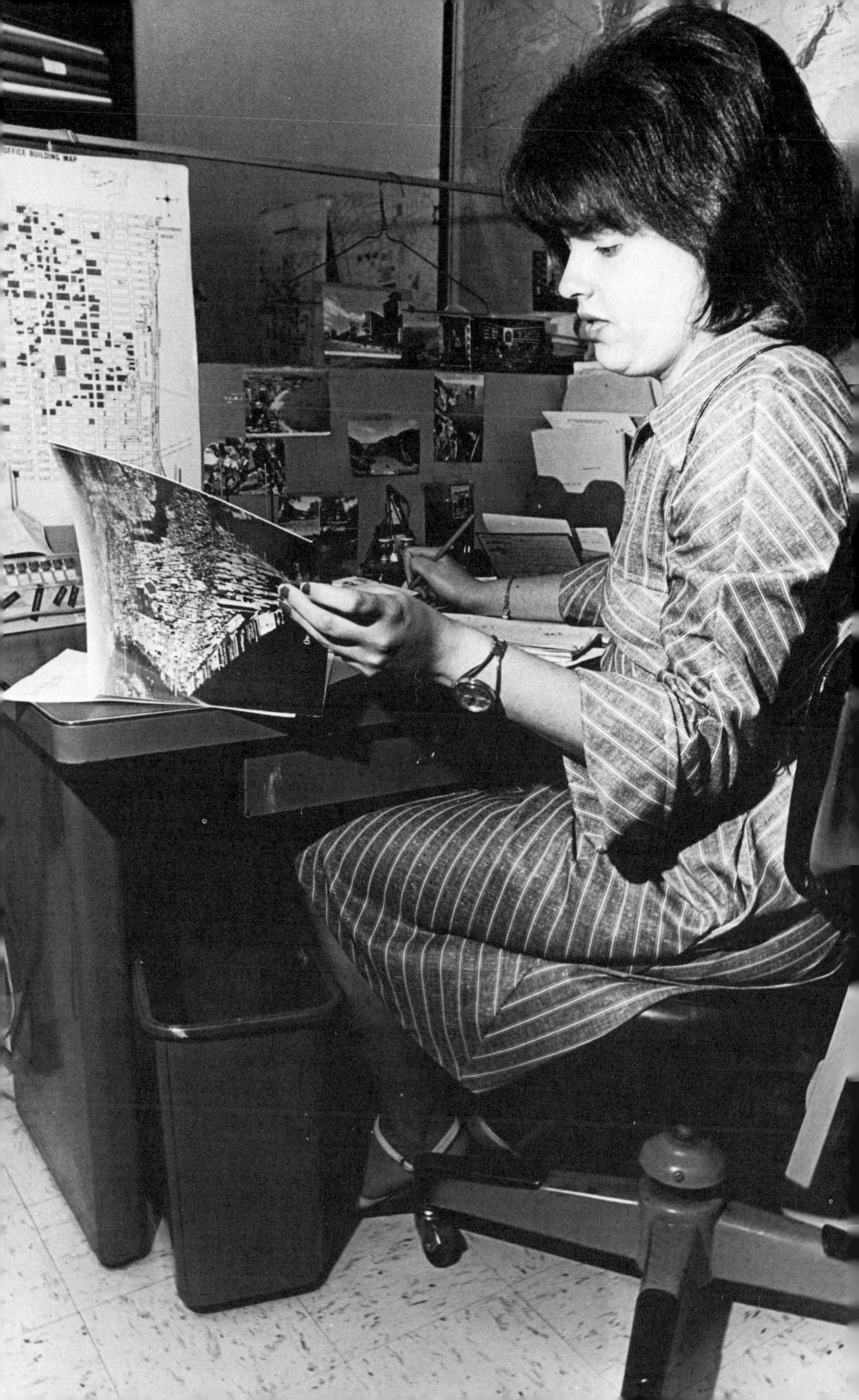
OFFICE BUILDING MAP

at 7 percent nationwide. This amount is generally divided between the broker and the salesperson. Usually, neither receives a set salary. An experienced salesperson or broker in a large city might earn anywhere from $7,500 to $40,000 a year in commissions. Earnings for a beginning salesperson or broker would be much lower. A broker dealing in commercial properties might make a commission of 3½ percent on a $2 million sale. A broker handling residential properties might make similar commissions on sales ranging from $30,000 to $100,000. But, of course, the residential broker will undoubtedly be selling more properties.

## Sales

A real estate salesperson may or may not need a license. (Check with your local realty board to find out the requirements in your state.) He or she usually works for a broker (discussed in the previous chapter). However, many real estate salespeople later become brokers themselves.

Not everyone is born to be a salesperson. It is generally agreed in all sections of the responsible real estate industry that the best salespeople for any type of property are the "soft" salespeople. Property isn't just a commodity that can, or should, be forced on the buyer. There are the "hard" salespeople in real estate, pushing and shoving for a sale irrespective of whether or not the buyer is really happy. But that isn't the way most responsible brokers work. And when you go to work as a salesperson, you must be sure that you have picked a brokerage house that isn't going to demand that you use work methods you don't enjoy or approve of.

On the other hand, you have to be careful not to soft-sell yourself out of a sale! People new to selling have been known to lose a sale on a house because they let the crucial moment pass when they should have said to the prospective buyer: "Well, Ms. Fortunoff, from what you say about the house, and from what you told me beforehand about your and your family's needs, this seems like just the right house for you, and in the right neighborhood. How about buying it?" The buyer must always be *sold* a house, or he or she may drift on with no sale resulting.

Here are some of the things a prospective employer will tell you when you go for an interview. You will not be paid a salary, but you will work as a "contracted employee" on a straight commission basis. The exact commission will vary from broker to broker, but generally you will be paid 50 percent of the broker's fee, which usually averages 7 percent of the purchase price. The higher the purchase price, the lower the commission percentage.

In his excellent book *Real Estate Brokerage,* Frederick E. Case gives a checklist for employers to use when they are interviewing a prospective salesperson. The questions below are based on the ones he mentions. Being aware of what you will be asked and how you will be judged will definitely help you get the job.

1. *Speaking ability.* Is the interviewee articulate—able to express himself or herself freely and coherently?

2. *Personality.* Is the interviewee outgoing or does the interviewer have to "dig" to find out what sort of person the interviewee is?

3. *How hard will he/she work?* This is tough for the interviewer to gauge accurately. If you can give the interviewer some solid facts about the kind of schedule

you maintained in high school or college, it will be a great help.

4. *Aggression.* Do you, the job-seeker, take a leading role in the conversation, without being hostile or pushy? Do you open up new topics for discussion, or do you wait passively to be asked questions?

5. *Judgment.* The interviewer will want to know how quickly you can size up a situation. This is an all-important trait for a salesperson. Job experience can help here, particularly in the retail business section. Were you a check-out clerk at the supermarket? Could you smell shoplifters a mile off?

6. *Manners.* Are they good without being over-effusive?

7. *Appearance.* You should be neatly and appropriately dressed.

8. *Honesty.* This is all-important in the real estate field. You will be asked to provide character references to a prospective employer. A broker is ultimately responsible for what the salespeople do and will want to be sure he or she is hiring a thoroughly honest person.

9. *Previous experience.* If you have had previous jobs, then you will need to provide references, and to be able to tell your prospective employer exactly how your past experience fits in with the job he or she has in mind.

If you have not had a job before, then you should have read up on all the available literature on selling, and on selling real estate in particular, and you will have to make positive remarks about yourself and your attitude about selling that will help your prospective employer decide whether or not you are a "good risk."

10. *Age.* In terms of selling real estate, twenty-five-plus is the most "acceptable" age for a junior salesperson. But if you're twenty and raring to go, start off with an office job with a broker. This is a way to learn the business, and it is time well spent. In every area of real estate

selling, buyers would be put off by an extremely young person selling them a house or whatever the property may be. If you can't get a job with a broker, then go into a business that is allied to real estate. Insurance is a good example.

11. *Automobile.* For a salesperson, a fairly new car is a must. It is part of "appearance," and it should be in good condition. You often have to drive people out to view properties, and if you have a dusty old jalopy, your prospective buyer isn't going to arrive at the property in the right frame of mind at all! A neat, clean, well-maintained car is essential.

12. *Marital status.* When you go for an interview as a salesperson, you must consider that your entire family is being interviewed too. Many brokers make a point of interviewing the husband or wife of the prospective employee. A good marriage is thought to be a great help toward success. Even if you don't agree with this, you should be aware that it may have influence.

13. *Financial status.* An interviewer will want to know all about your financial status, so you must be prepared to "tell all!" You may have to support yourself with savings for the first six months until the commissions start coming in, and the interviewer will want to be assured that you can maintain a reasonable standard of living during that time. He or she may ask to see *proof* that you can. Be prepared to open your bank records to your prospective employer.

14. *Activities, contacts.* These, as we have said already, are the keys to success in sales. What are you involved in? Are you coaching the Little League? Are you working with the Girl Scouts? Are you doing volunteer work with the aged? Are you an active member of your church? Of what organizations are you an officer? If you belong to an organization, that can mean sales. Everyone you know can mean sales.

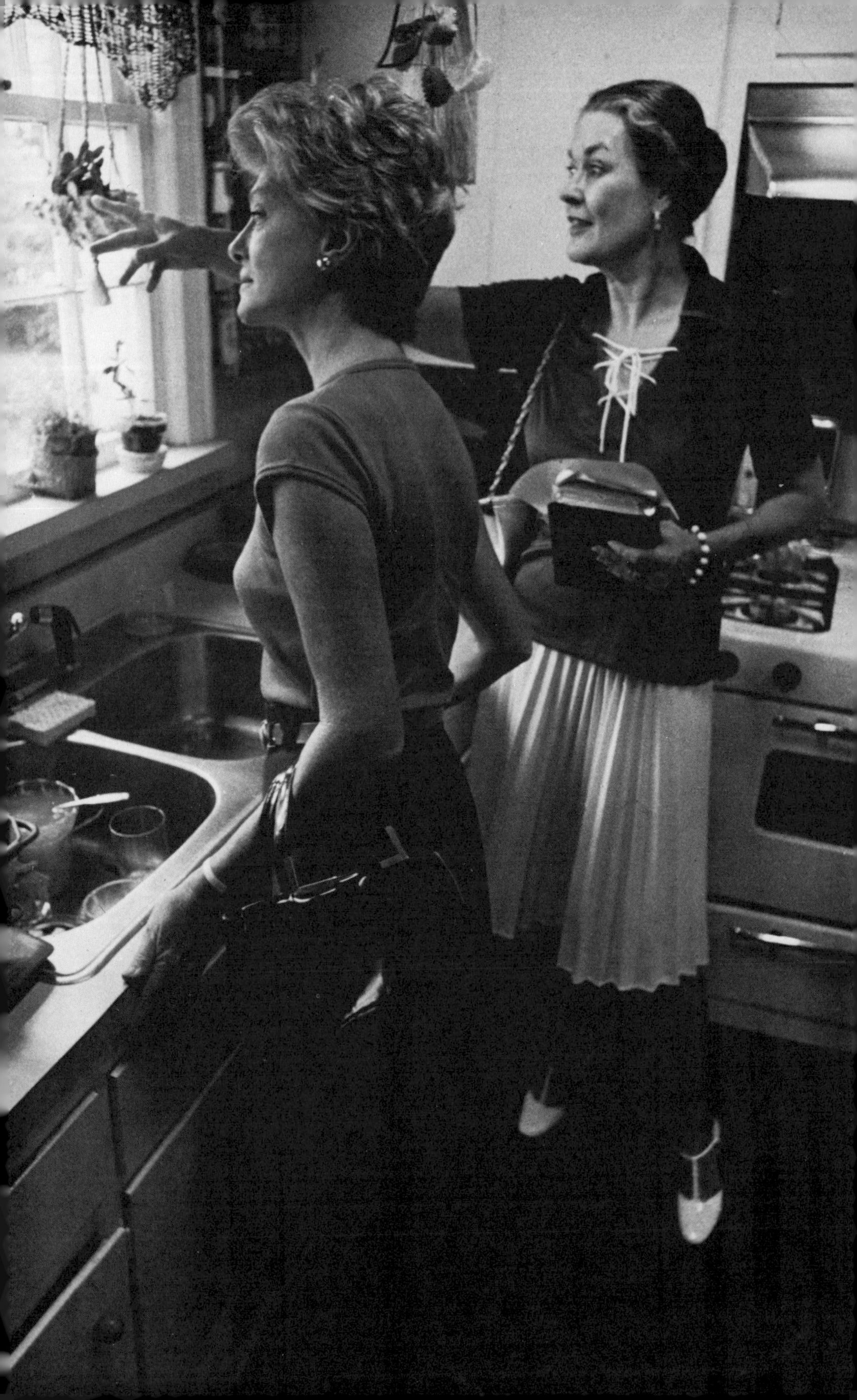

## RESIDENTIAL SELLING

Women are moving into real estate selling in greater numbers every year. Joan D. is a typical salesperson who lives and works in a suburban area outside an Eastern city of medium size.

Joan feels that being a woman is an advantage in selling real estate, particularly residential selling. "When I look at a house, I see how it can be *used*," she says. "I see a 'machine for living.' When I show a man or a woman the kitchen, I can point to the defects as well as to the advantages, and suggest ways the defects can be remedied. This comes out of *personal* experience. It isn't something I learned to do for professional reasons."

We asked Joan how she dealt with the problem of showing a house that had definite defects.

"Of course I point them out," she said, "but only in terms of how they can be remedied. And of course I push the good points first. That's part of being successful. But I make sure that poor points are brought to the buyer's attention; I don't want an unhappy buyer. It's bad for business. You see, selling real estate is really a question of reaching the best possible compromise. Human beings aren't perfect, so naturally they *will* build imperfect houses. The truly perfect house for a family would have to be specially designed and built for them. When people look for a house, there are always going to be things that aren't exactly the way they want. So, as I say, it is a compromise, and it is up to the salesperson to match the family to the best house for their needs.

"Now take a couple with two teen-age children. The first question I'm going to ask is: are the kids going to college? If so, are they going to a nearby college (in

**A definite asset to any kitchen—
a sunny window—is being
pointed out by this agent.**

which case they may be living at home)? Or are they going to a college at the other end of the state? If the first is true, the family will need a house that is big enough for a couple and two other adults. If the second is the case, the parents won't want a great barn of a house for just the two of them.

"I live in this neighborhood. I've been in the position recently of selling two properties on nearby streets. Now the people who moved in are close neighbors. Of course I want them to feel as good as possible about what they've bought."

## COMMERCIAL AND INDUSTRIAL SELLING

You are going to be dealing with a completely different set of problems if you sell commercial or industrial properties.

Let us take the case of a manufacturing company that has outgrown its present space. Alex O. is a salesperson who specializes in the industrial side of the real estate business. "There are an incredible number of questions to be asked and answered when a company is looking for new premises. I find I have to really research a business I am unfamiliar with to find out the basic information. I do this even before I go and talk to the people at the company to find out the *particular* needs they have. Take water supply. Some manufacturers may not only need a lot of water, but they may need water of a special chemical composition. Another company may need water in great quantities, and you've got to be sure when you show the premises that the manufacturer can get water not only this year and next year but five or ten years hence. So you've really got to know all about the distribution and availability of water for industrial uses in the area. And you can't fudge something like that. You've got to be sure.

"You've got to give a corporation a complete picture. The more solid facts you have ready when you sit down at the first meeting, the more pleased they are going to be. You are going to have to know a lot about the company itself. How long has it been in business? Is this the only plant, or is their main plant elsewhere? Is it a privately owned company, or is it publicly owned? If an industrial facility is moving into a new area, you can also help them with information on skilled and unskilled workers available in the area. If there are insufficient skilled workers, and they need them for a few months at a time each year, then you may be able to bring in one of your colleagues (if you work for a larger brokerage firm) to set up a trailer park to house the skilled workers coming in and out of the area. Or perhaps a company will need apartments, and houses too. You've got to be ready to give them complete real estate service. If you don't there'll be half a dozen salespeople right behind you who will!"

## ON THE JOB

**How do you get listings?**
The multiple-listing system mentioned earlier is used mainly by brokers selling residential properties. In the other specialties, part of your job as a salesperson is to get listings of properties for the brokerage. Frederick Case lists the following as methods he found successful in getting listings. But keep in mind that there is no one set of methods that covers all types of real estate.

1. *Former clients.* They recommend the salesperson and/or brokerage to friends or acquaintances who either want to buy or sell.

2. *Responses to newspaper advertising.* Part of your job as a salesperson will involve writing ads for properties.

3. *Public relations activities in the community.* The salesperson joins community groups and gains a reputation in town for being involved in such organizations as the Little League, the volunteer fire department, the tennis club, the church, and so on.

4. *Telephone calls.* Calls come in from people who need help in buying or selling and have been directed to the office by means of methods 1, 2, and 3.

5. *Office visitors, the drop-in trade.* These are people who see the realtor's sign and decide to walk into the office and make inquiries or register their needs.

6. *Door-to-door soliciting.* If a salesperson sees a "For Sale" sign on a house, he or she will then either telephone other homeowners on the block or knock on their doors and ask whether they too are thinking of selling—or buying.

7. *"For Sale by Owner" signs.* A salesperson can often convince a homeowner that using a trained real estate salesperson to handle the sale is going to be simpler and involve fewer problems than "going it alone."

8. *Direct mail.* Salespeople are expected to prepare mailing pieces, with details of the property and photographs attractively arranged. These are sent out to potential clients.

9. *TV, radio, and other signs on property.*

Remember: a courteous, pleasant, helpful salesperson is always remembered. You may not make a sale this time, but five years later you will.

**The woman on the right, an experienced saleswoman, is training a junior salesperson to use the various real estate directories.**

[28]

& MORTGAGES RECORDED
to SUPPLEMENT No. 24
1976 to JANUARY 15, 1977
COUNTY REAL ESTATE DIRECTORY

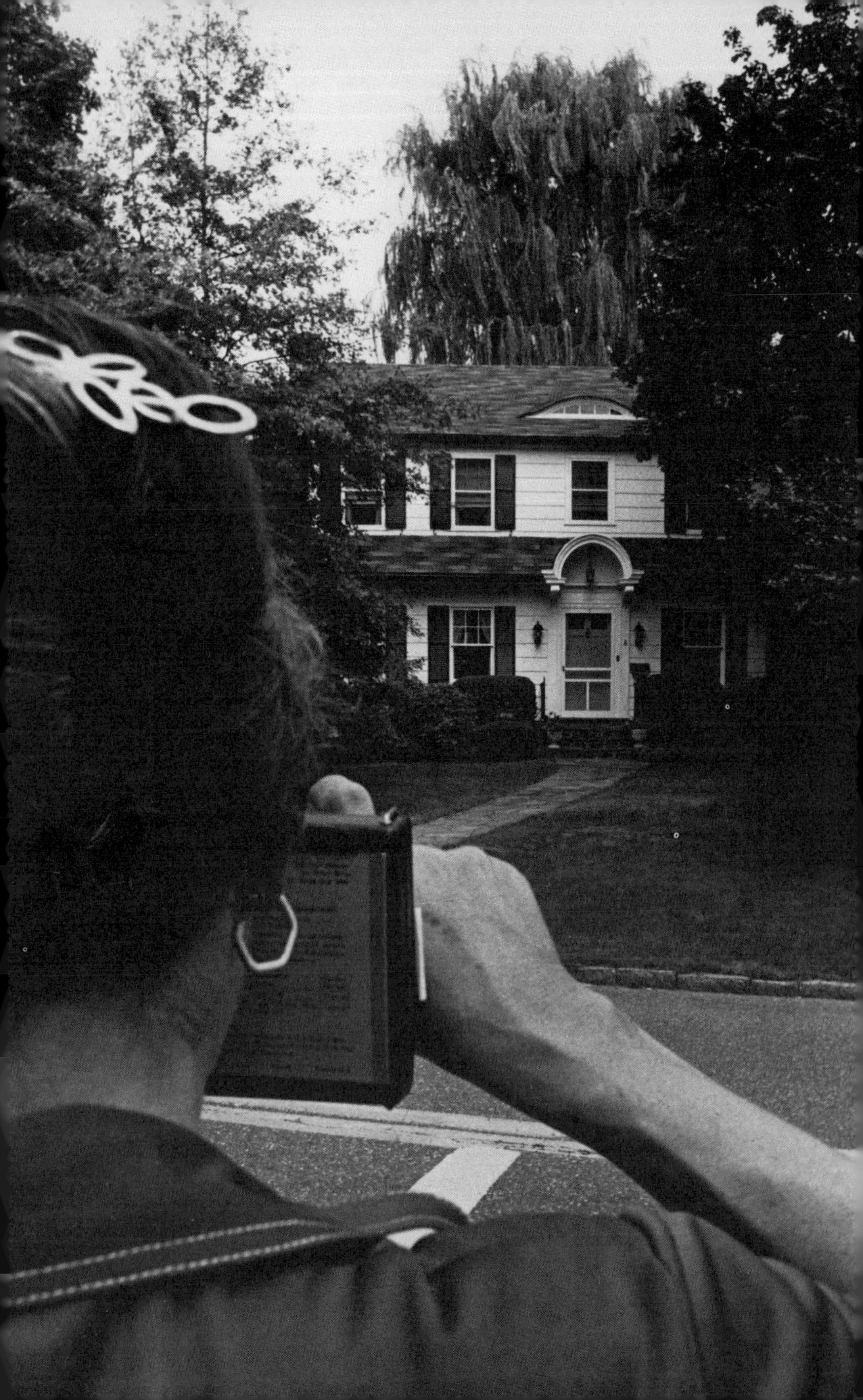

**Work habits**
Most brokerages will have a policy book which sets out the dos and don'ts: office hours, manners, dress, code of ethics. You will be expected to keep it with you and to abide by it. In addition, you will need to keep a handbook, a loose-leaf binder containing the following items:

1. Prospect file.
2. All the forms you need for a closing (official completion of a sale).
3. A file of current listings.
4. Information on neighborhood facilities.
5. Maps.
6. Information on financing (loans, etc.).
7. An up-to-date list of recent sales.
8. Details of the property or properties you are showing.

Most brokers also have property check-lists for use by their salespeople so that every item of importance can be inspected and assessed: plumbing, electrical wiring, floors, walls, roof.

**The documents**
When a property is transferred from one person to another, there is a bundle of paper involved. These are the main documents you will be handling:

1. *Deed to the property.* This shows ownership.

**The agent is photographing a house for sale. The finished picture may then be used on a bulletin board display in the waiting room of the real estate office or included in a mailing brochure.**

2. *Mortgage deed.* If you are buying a home, and you have borrowed money to do so from a savings and loan organization, the mortgage deed is the legal document that sets out the details of the transaction, for example how much money has been loaned, at what annual interest, and how many years it will take to pay back the loan.

3. *Note or bond.* This will be for the cash amount, the down payment that the buyer is making.

4. *Title insurance.* This insures the buyer in case it is later found that the seller did not have title to the property.

**Knowledge of the construction industry**

Since the construction of buildings, whatever they are, lies at the very center of the real estate industry, it is important to mention briefly some of the ways in which the broker or salesperson gets involved.

As has been said throughout this book, a real estate professional cannot know too much about his or her chosen area. And knowledge of the construction industry is very important indeed. If a salesperson sells a house, and the kitchen needs remodeling or the house needs new siding, then the buyers are going to need expert advice in selecting a contractor, especially if they are new to the neighborhood. And to give truly expert advice the broker or salesperson must know the contractors in the area well. They must give the buyer several names for estimates and be able to tell the buyer that contractor X may seem more expensive than contractor Y, but he does a better job.

Many contractors specialize. There are some who specialize in plumbing–heating–air conditioning, some in painting–paperhanging–decorating, others in electrical work, still others in masonry and other stonework, and so on. Further, there are heavy construction contractors, highway and street construction contractors, and general building contractors. As a real estate person, you had better know exactly what contractor does what type of work and how well.

If you are a broker or salesperson selling land to people who want to build a vacation home, then they too are going to need information on contractors.

**Contacts with developers**
A developer is an individual or company who subdivides land into lots and builds and sells houses, factories, hotels, skyscrapers, etc., to customers. The developer is an important contact for anyone working in residential real estate, and an alert broker or salesperson will keep in close contact with developers in the area.

**Contacts with architects**
Architects are important contacts for the real estate person in any community. Because they are responsible for the design of a building, they will be almost the first to know when new construction is planned.

**Contacts with engineers**
Engineers are another source of information. They can, for example, give a real estate broker or salesperson an early warning on pending highway construction. The state may provide funds for a highway that is planned to plow straight through an older neighborhood of two-family homes, but actually work may be suspended indefinitely because of the condition of the economy or because the state wants to channel highway money into mass transit instead. Will the highway be built? And if not, how is the real estate standing in its path affected by the indecision?

# Management

A property manager is first and foremost a diplomat. He or she must negotiate with people who want to rent their homes, arrange deals with people looking for factories or commercial premises, or perhaps find investors for a condominium. The property manager has become increasingly important in all aspects of the real estate industry since the depression of the 1930s.

Before the depression, most property was owned by individuals. But with the stock market crash of 1929, individual ownership dropped considerably and control of buildings went to banks, insurance companies, savings societies, trust companies, and investment protective committees. Increasingly, again, professional people—doctors, lawyers, accountants—want to invest money in real estate, and they need property managers to handle the properties for them. Property management is a business, and the property manager is a highly trained and experienced professional.

What kind of person succeeds as a property manager? One who is able to deal with people of every economic level, for one thing. As a property manager, you must be able to get along with the president of a large corporation, the head of a labor union, and the people who do maintenance work in a building.

You must know the buildings you are managing inside out. If you are managing a commercial building, for example, you must be familiar with the kind of work elevator maintenance people do, so that you can keep an eye on whether or not it is being done properly. You must be able to read blueprints, so that you can tell a prospective tenant what can and cannot be done in the way of construction in the space they want to rent.

You must be a public relations expert, a promoter. Most buildings cannot afford to employ a professional advertising agency, so it is the manager who must figure out ways of letting people know that the building has space for rent—via newspaper advertising, signs on the property, or perhaps TV and radio ads on local stations.

Above all, you must be an expert in the future. The manager of a building must be able to set rents not only for this year but for next year too. Which way is the market going, up or down?

One thing all managers agree upon: there is no ultimate "How to Manage a Building for Fun and Profit" manual that will tell a manager exactly how to manage a particular property. Every neighborhood is different. Buildings may have traits in common, but every building is unique in its position on the street, the district it is in, and the kind of tenants it hopes to attract.

Successful property management has been described as "an art that relies heavily on the psychology of human relations." And a successful manager must be much more than a businessperson. He or she must be experienced in the real estate industry, a community person. Owners, tenants, employees, service people, labor unions—all of them must be dealt with, and their differences must be resolved without rubbing anybody the wrong way.

A property manager must be an expert in the local zoning laws too, and he or she must know all state and city plans for the area where the building being managed is located.

Handling insurance for a building is yet another part of a property manager's business. A manager must be able to estimate the risks involved in the writing of insurance for tenants and the general public. For example,

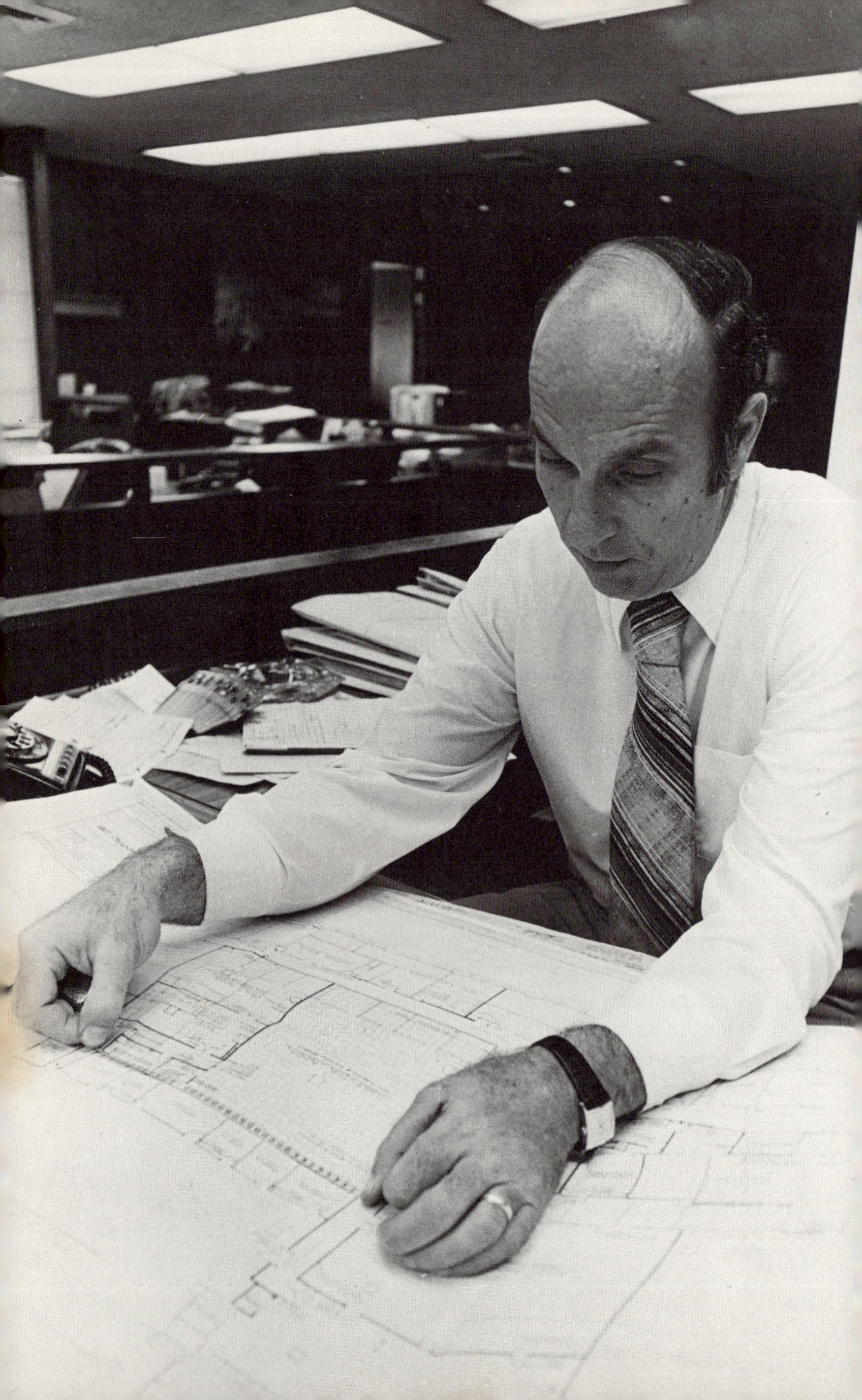

when discussing insurance with a manufacturer of buttons, the manager must be familiar with the materials used and must know if any change in materials is planned during the term of the policy. If it is, then the new materials must be included in the policy for full coverage.

The manager most commonly represents the interests of the buyer of insurance (the tenant, for example). The insurance broker seeks out the insurance company that seems to offer the best coverage for the broker's client. The insurance company then pays the broker a commission. But the broker is still the representative of the *buyer*. An insurance *agency* represents the insurance company. It is common practice for property managers to start off representing clients as insurance brokers, and then when business has been built up, the managers become insurance agents. But insurance is an entirely separate business from property management.

The manager involved in insurance underwriting must have an extensive knowledge of insurance and know how and where to shop around and what to look for. The manager must know what type of labor is employed, the physical risks involved in the work, the average number of workers employed, and must keep abreast of new forms of coverage.

A manager who is involved in insurance underwriting must keep detailed and accurate records. Even when the insurance is underwritten by some other agency, the manager of a building must have copies of all insurance

**An employee in the maintenance department of a large management company is working on plans for interior reconstruction work. Several construction companies will later bid for the project.**

policies that affect the building in any way. Insurance is yet another way that he or she must *know* the building. There must be regular inspections of offices, elevators, stairways, plumbing, and electrical fixtures. If faulty wiring causes a fire, for example, and there has not been the periodic inspection required by the insurance policy, then coverage may be canceled altogether.

Most property managers are partners in, or employees of, management companies. These companies are hired to manage larger buildings and to deal with the many different people we've mentioned earlier—owners, tenants, etc. In short, when someone owns a building but doesn't want to run it, he or she will contact a property management company to take charge.

Some property managers work instead for large corporations. Let's say the corporation Bluebird decides to build because it is cramped in its present building or buildings. It decides early on to build a bigger building than needed right away, because it can rent the extra space to other businesses for the time being. A property manager on the payroll would have to decide what type of tenant to look for and what length of lease to offer. Offices are generally long-term tenants. Nobody wants to heave the files around every six months, and moving is an expensive business. But the manager of Bluebird's building has to bear in mind that the space must not be tied up so far ahead that Bluebird will be unable to make use of it if it wants to. A large corporation will generally know where it is headed, and the manager will have guidance in planning. Perhaps he or she will know beforehand that ten years is the maximum period of time

**This part-owner building manager is checking on the rewiring job the electrician just finished.**

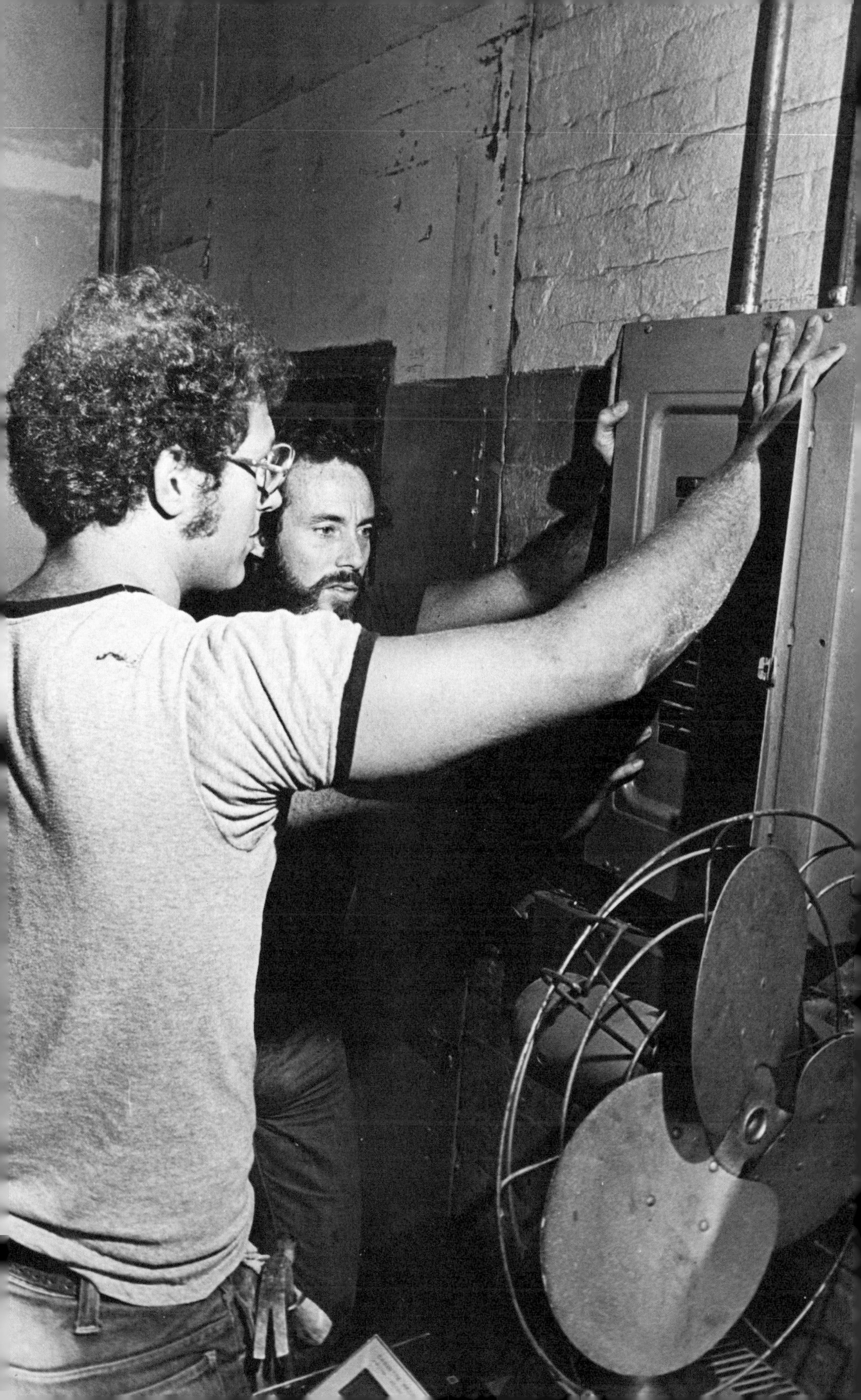

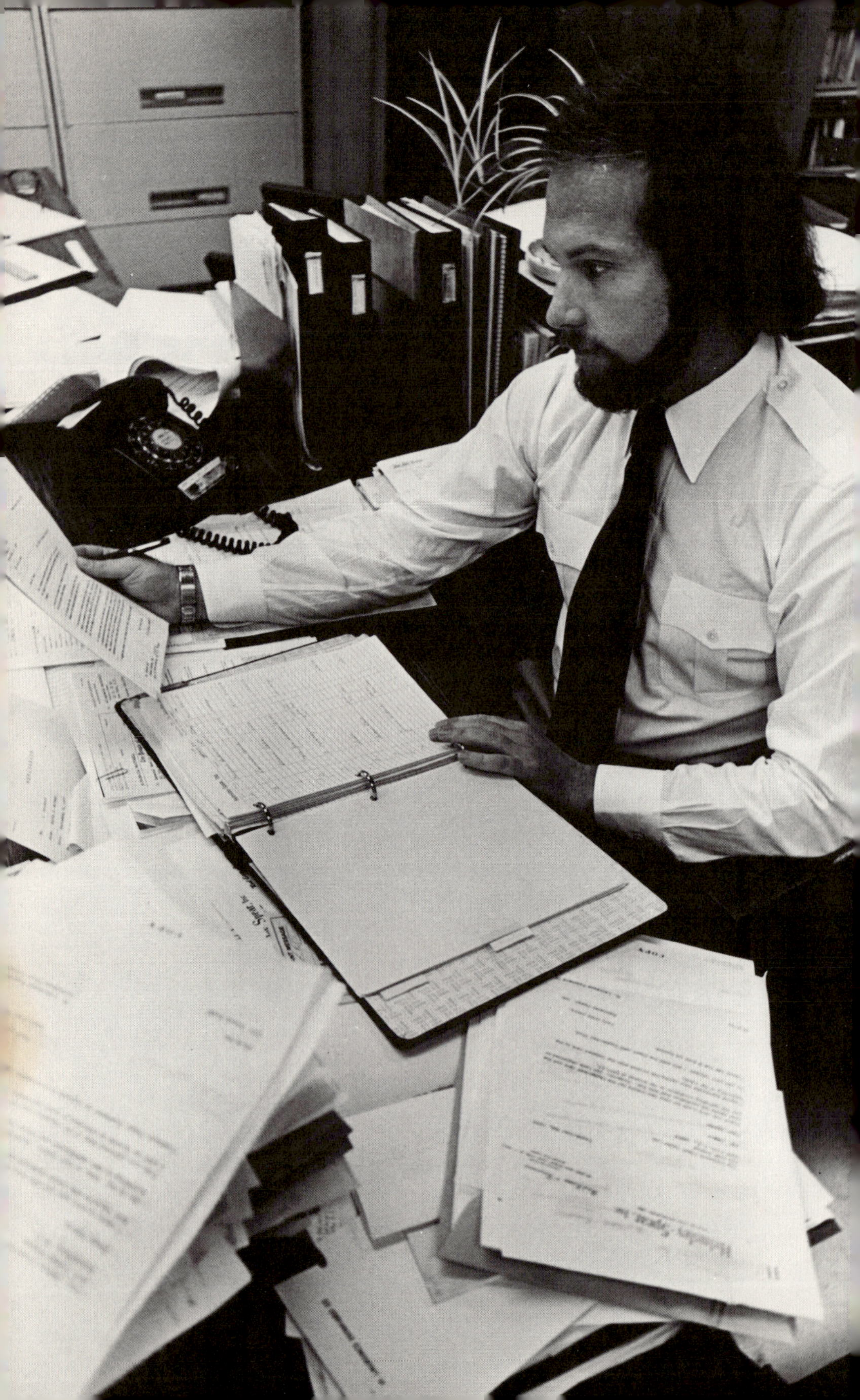

the space should be rented out. Then the question might be, should the space be rented to a tenant who will sign a ten-year lease or to a tenant who will sign a five-year lease? Five years could well be more profitable. The property manager will have an idea of inflation trends and be able to fix the leases accordingly.

George H., a property manager of many years' experience says, "Yes, you've got to learn the ins and outs of so many different types of businesses, you'd be amazed. Only this morning I was talking to a guy who wanted to open a plant store. Well, this is a growing business. It seems as though everybody's buying plants. Still, I'd never had to deal with that type of business before. After the guy had called me, I settled down to find out what I could about it. And by the time we sat down to discuss it, I was able to ask him pertinent questions. Now I've got a new tenant for that store, and I've got a head full of information about a new business.

"I couldn't begin to tell you the different subjects I've got to deal with. This is a big building, forty floors. If something goes wrong with the plumbing, I know what the problem is likely to be, simply because I have a picture of the building's plumbing in the back of my mind. You're going to spend a lot of money if the plumber has to start groping around."

There are innumerable kinds of buildings that need property managers: apartment buildings, apartment hotels, medical buildings, the older mart buildings where manufacturers and jobbers rent space to show their goods to wholesale buyers. There are restaurants and bars that create their own particular headaches.

**Going over tenant-payment records is a large part of this building manager's job.**

There are buildings like the John Hancock in Chicago, where the manager must deal with "mixed-use"—apartments, offices, and stores, all in the same building.

There are property managers in the hotel and motel industry, and that is a whole specialty in itself.

There are mobile home parks near military installations; there are mobile home parks near industrial plants, where skilled workers are brought in for limited periods of time for special jobs.

Charley D. is a property manager specializing in apartment buildings in a New England city. He says, "We've had our booms in construction, and sometimes we've been cursed with an over-boom so that apartment space has been coming out of our ears. You've got a problem when that happens: how to attract new tenants, how to make your building the place to rent in town. It's very competitive around here. You've got to be able to deal with the lean years when the economy is down, and you've got to be ready with a plan for the future when the economy recovers. There is no such thing in this business as a plateau. But I thrive on the complexities, the problems to be solved. Take labor relations. As the manager of a building, I've got to strike a balance between the owner's interests and the unions' demands. The union guys I deal with are serious. They know how far they can push for their membership. I've got an obligation to the owner to get the best deal I can. The union has an obligation to its membership to get the best deal it can. We have more in common than anything else. It isn't in labor's interest to put the owner out of business by unrealistic demands, and it isn't in the owner's interest

**An apartment building manager discussing lease terms with a prospective tenant.**

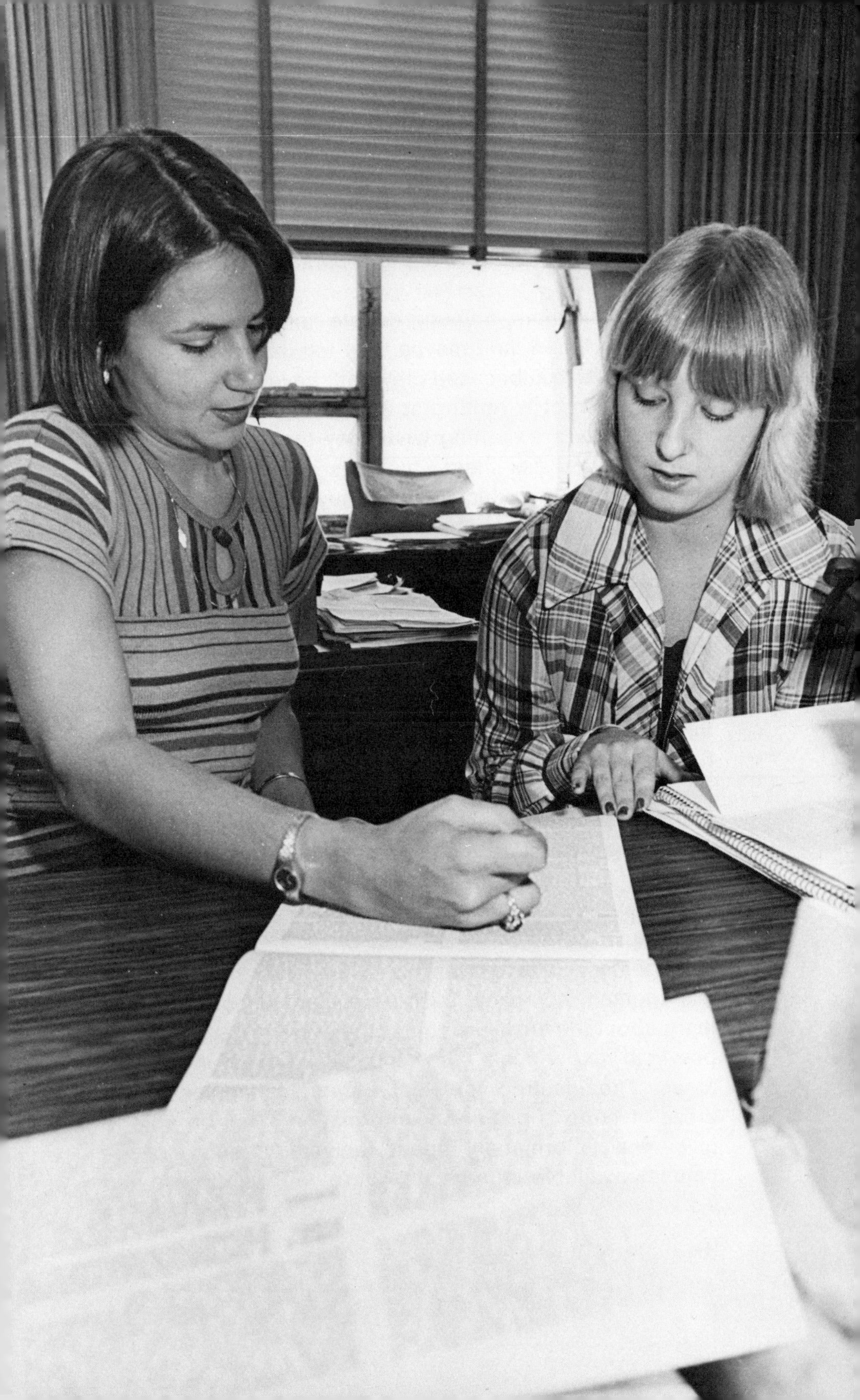

to cut labor's throat. This is where you come to the key to successful property management.

"You see, this is a human business first, last, and foremost. You have to relate to a person's needs as a human being.

"For example, a young couple comes to me looking for an apartment, and maybe they tell me they're earning a total of $15,000 because they both have jobs. The apartment they want is renting at $300 a month, which is fine if they really are earning what they claim to be earning. But when you ask them—and this happened to me recently—about the kind of work they do, and you realize that they may be netting around $10,000, then you wonder about them. Are they a good risk? They're over twenty-one. No one can tell them not to spend more than a certain amount on a place to live. But suppose one of them loses a job? Then the rent isn't only going to be a burden; it's going to be a downright impossibility.

"On the other hand, you get the feeling sometimes that even if they are exaggerating, it won't be long before they're earning that $15,000. So you take a chance."

Salaries for property managers range from $10,000 in the most junior levels to $40,000 to $50,000. Most property managers start off as real estate salespeople or brokers, and then specialize in property management after they have had a number of years of experience in the industry. The other method of getting into property management is to get an entry-level job in a property management company, such as a clerical position, then learn about the business during the evenings and back up practical experience with college courses in related areas. The Institute for Real Estate Management (address given in "For Further Information") will be able to give you information about university and college courses available in the state where you wish to live and work.

For property managers of many years' experience, the Institute for Real Estate Management offers courses and very stiff examinations that lead to the designation of Certified Property Manager. The Institute has established a tough code of ethics to govern the behavior of its nearly 5,000 member brokers.

# Appraisal

Although appraisal (deciding property value) is a part of the broker's, salesperson's, and manager's job, in a sense it is a specialized occupation in itself.

How much is it worth? That is the basic question asked about real estate, and the professional appraiser is trained to answer that question. Besides having an eye for the details of the interior of a building—flooring, walls, plumbing, ceiling, wiring, etc.—the appraiser must take into consideration the place where the building is located. What is the size of the building, the shape? What kind of a street is it on? What kind of a neighborhood is it in?

In a residential area, is a big old house sitting on a skinny plot of land? If so, how does it affect the value? In terms of agricultural land, the composition of the soil is very important. Potatoes grow better in one kind of soil than in another. You don't try to grow potatoes in soil that is better suited to citrus fruit. Soil is important in a different sense in the downtown area of a city. In the middle of a construction boom, suppose a big new oil well has opened up nearby. Is the downtown area marshy, and if so, how far down do you have to dig to reach bedrock? This can govern the type of building erected on a piece of land, whether it is a high-rise or not. Is the land flat, or is it hilly? Obviously it is easier to build on flat land, and cheaper too.

What about zoning? Is there likely to be a change in the zoning laws that will affect the value of the property adversely?

In appraising the value of a home, not only is the economic state of the neighborhood taken into consideration—is it going up or is it going down—but also what are the prices of comparable houses nearby? Whenever a property changes hands, an appraisal must be made by a trained person. Many large real estate brokerages have a certified appraiser on staff.

If you are interested in becoming an appraiser, you probably should start your career as a real estate broker or salesperson and gain practical experience in the real estate industry over a period of at least five years. The University of Wisconsin, for one, offers a master's program in valuation, and the NATIONAL ASSOCIATION OF REALTORS® (as well as the other appraisal organizations listed in "For Further Information") will be glad to send you information about universities, colleges, and community colleges offering courses in real estate and appraisal. The Canadian Real Estate Association will have information on Canada.

Although degrees in real estate are invaluable, so too are degrees in business administration, architecture, law, engineering, or sociology. Practical experience in the fields of accounting, property management, and building inspection are also recommended.

To become successful in a career in appraisal, you will need a good head for figures, analytical ability, and a

**A land appraiser checking soil content.**

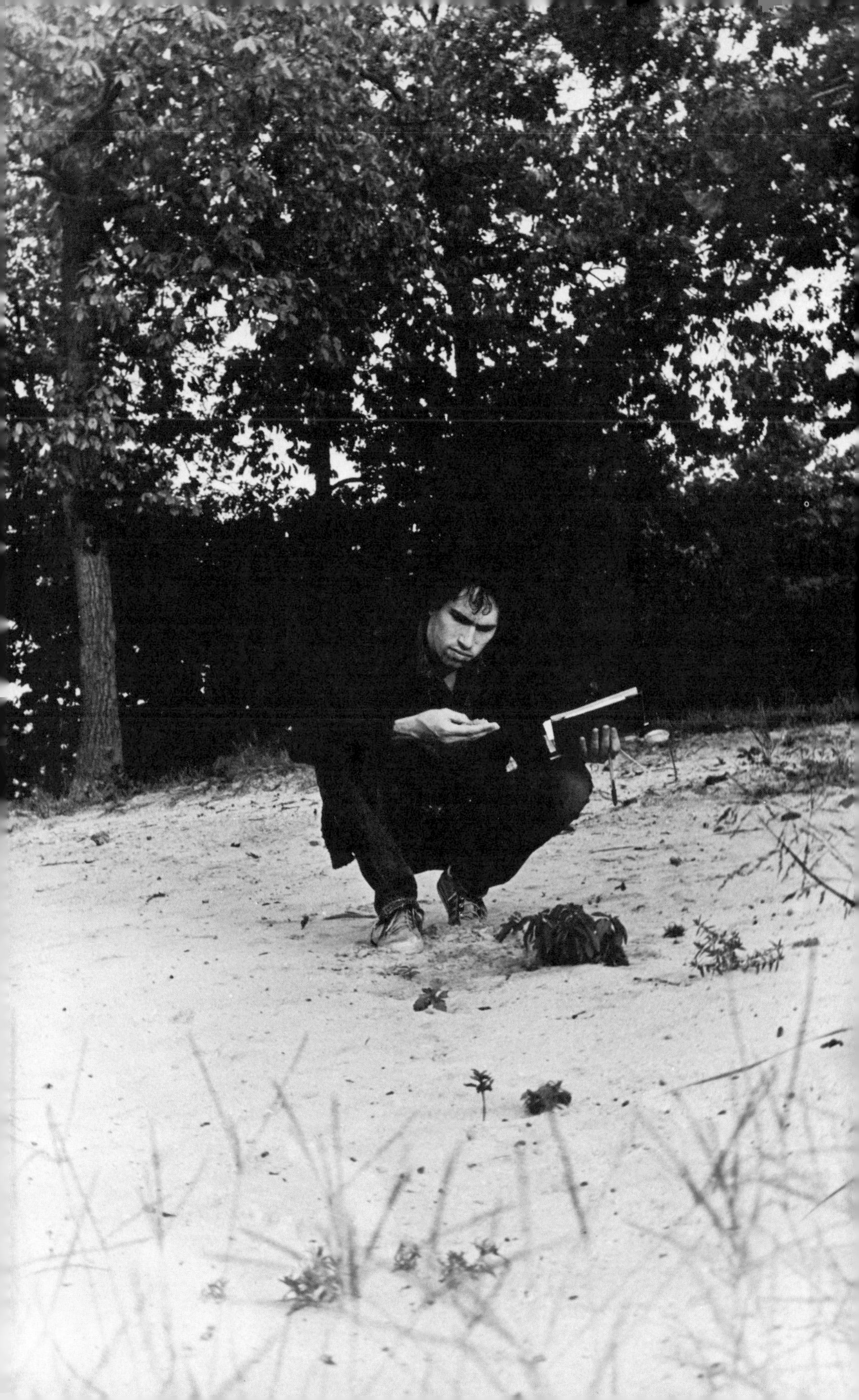

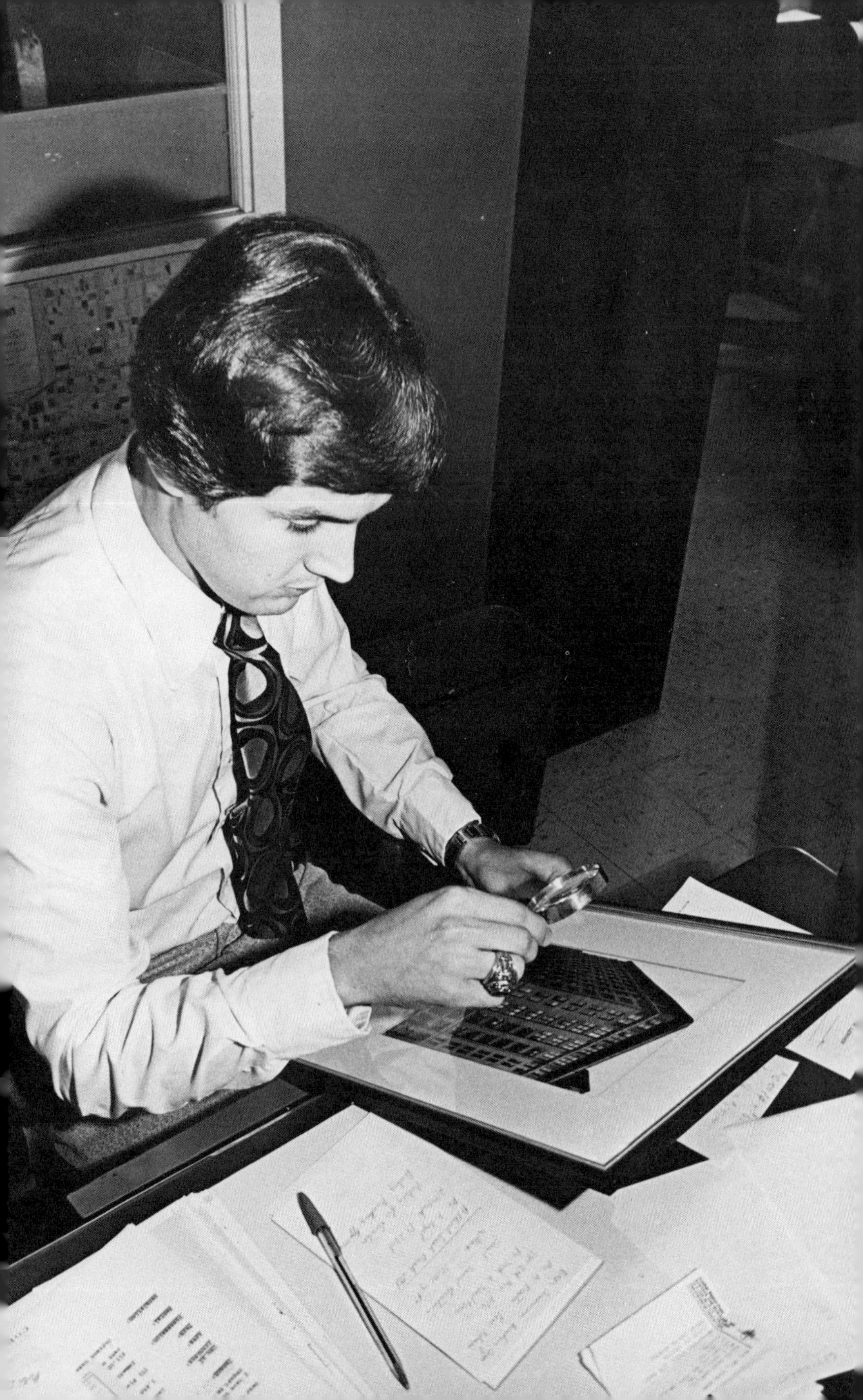

thorough knowledge of the principles underlying land use, financing, construction, zoning, and taxation. Also, you will probably want to become "certified." To do so, you will have to pass a stiff examination and have a good amount of on-the-job experience.

The federal government also employs a number of appraisers. If you work for the government, you can expect to earn between $900 and $1400 a month. Self-employed appraisers can earn between $14,000 and $30,000 a year. Salaries are somewhat lower in Canada.

# Investment

According to *Webster's,* to invest means "to commit money for a long period in order to earn a financial return." If you put your money in a savings bank, you are investing, but the value of your money can be eaten away by inflation. If you buy a house, you are investing your money in real estate, and it is better protected from inflation.

Investing money in real estate is known as "equity investment." This means that if you invest $100,000 in a building, you do so in order to preserve the money at more or less its original level. In terms of the real estate market, which is generally on the rise, you may well in-

**This building appraiser is using photographs to check for possible structural defects in a building his client is considering buying.**

crease the $100,000 over the years. But your main motive was to put the money in "a safe place," to protect it from inflation.

Many openings for real estate investors can be found in the real estate investment departments of banks or insurance companies. Both of these kinds of institutions have training programs and will often assist employees who wish to continue their education (for example, to study for a master's or a doctoral degree). Some investment jobs are also available at savings and loan associations, which, since they are a major source of mortgages, require real estate investment experts to assess property the association may invest in. The government, too, has some investment openings (see chapter following).

Most of today's mortgage loans are made to provide the funding for a home, business, or industrial property. Mortgage "risk financing" is one of the top real estate specialties.

Much of the money for mortgage financing comes from insurance companies, who are large investors and need the services of real estate experts on their staffs to assess the soundness of investments. Such people recommend types of property best suited to the institution's investment needs.

## ON THE JOB

There are a number of things all investors must take into consideration before investing money in a particular property. The questions that follow are based on Jerome Gross's *Concise Desk Guide to Real Estate Practice and Procedure*. When you know how to deal with each of these areas, you will be in a position to succeed as an investor.

- [ ] How much income will the property produce *before* the expenses are deducted? (That is to say maintenance, insurance, etc.)
- [ ] What *are* the expenses?
- [ ] How much cash is needed to buy the property?
- [ ] How much income will be gotten from the property *after* all the expenses have been paid?
- [ ] How much does the value of the property *increase* each year?
- [ ] Is the structure of the building sound, and is it in good repair?
- [ ] Is the price being asked a realistic one? Is the building in question good value in terms of present real estate values?
- [ ] Are there hidden possibilities that do not show up on the balance sheet (for example, an adjacent lot for sale at a low price that would allow for future expansion)?
- [ ] What is the long-range outlook for the property? Is the area improving, or otherwise?
- [ ] Is your investment going to be helpful from a tax point of view, or is it going to be helpful in terms of income?

**REAL ESTATE INVESTMENT COUNSELING**

This is a new area in the real estate industry, and it is not the type of work you would consider until you had accumulated a considerable educational background in real estate, investment techniques, economics and finance, and had also accumulated years of practical experience, preferably as a broker, property manager, or appraiser. A real estate counselor is paid a fee based on the amount of work involved in researching an investment possibility. Because counseling is such a new field, there is no accurate information on annual earnings.

With the increasing complexity of the real estate market, more and more people are taking expert advice before they invest in land or buildings, so the counseling field is likely to expand over the years.

**EDUCATION AND EXPERIENCE**

A person who wants to enter the real estate investment field should probably have a bachelor's degree in business administration, economics, or real estate. An educational and work background in brokerage, appraisal, or property management is also recommended.

# Government Service

The United States contains a total of 2,271,000,000 acres of land, and a whopping 765,000,000 acres are under the direct supervision of the government.

If you want to get an idea of the numbers of *buildings* occupied by state, city, and federal government departments, take a look at your telephone directory. The listings for New York City alone take up four pages, and they include schools, libraries, prisons, day care centers, zoos, museums, health services, hospitals, public housing, fire houses, police stations, tax offices, the sanitation department, administrative offices dealing with buses and subways, courts, and many, many more. The federal government alone owns $141.3 billion worth of real property.

In 1975, 2,850,448 people were employed by government agencies, and when you think of the real estate involved in providing office space for the 1,894,000 white-collar workers alone you begin to understand what is involved.

The following U.S. government departments hire people for real estate jobs of one kind or another—property management, selling, investing, etc.

- Department of Agriculture
- Army Corps of Engineers
- Department of Commerce
- Bureau of the Census
- Bureau of Indian Affairs
- Bureau of Land Management
- Outdoor Recreation, Public Roads, Reclamation
- Farmers Home Administration
- Federal Aviation Administration
- Federal Home Loan Bank
- Federal Housing Administration
- Fish and Wildlife Service
- Forest Service
- General Services Administration
- Department of Housing and Urban Development
- Internal Revenue Service
- Justice Department
- National Park Service
- Navy Department
- Department of the Army

Post Office Department
Small Business Administration
Veterans Administration

(The Canadian Real Estate Association will be able to give you information regarding Canadian government departments using real estate professionals.)

At the city, state, and federal level, there are many departments involved in assessing real property for taxation purposes. They need appraisers to estimate the worth of property. Government appraisers should have a college degree, two to five years' experience, and should have passed the civil service exams.

There is also the whole area of public housing, which involves the management of buildings and the renting of apartments. Foreclosures for nonpayment of taxes make government the owners of huge numbers of houses and other real estate of every kind. When the various branches of government decide to sell such properties, then those sales must be handled by qualified personnel, just as sales of property are handled by a professional in the private sector. If the federal government becomes the proud owner of a large office building because the owner was unable to pay taxes, then that building will still require management. It will still need someone to oversee the renting of space, the supervision of maintenance personnel, and the arranging of insurance.

**Many government and nongovernment computer operators now work in the real estate industry.**

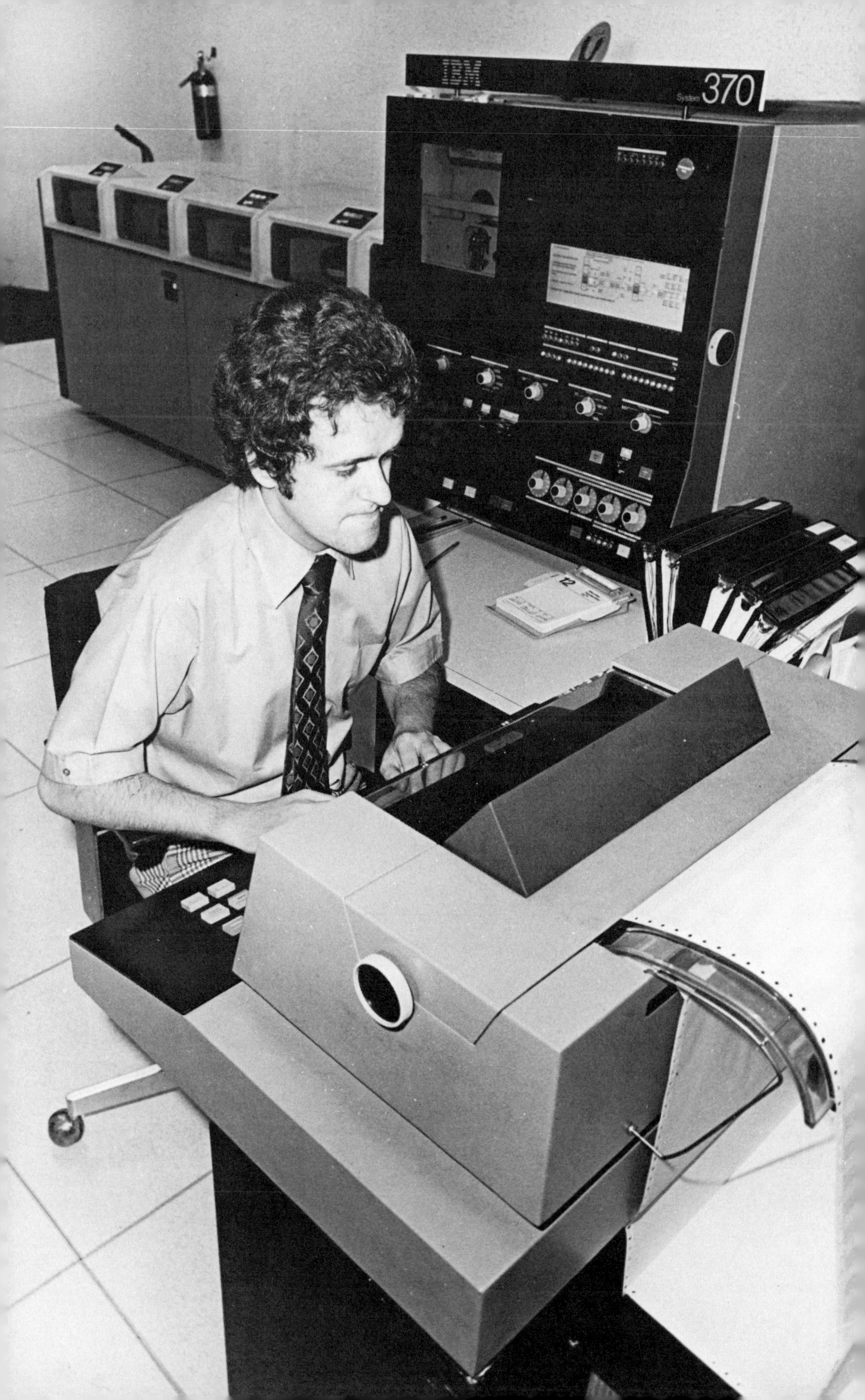
IBM
System 370

SHOPPING CENTER WORLD
REALTORS' Review
Real Estate Forum
building
AUGUST/1977
Forum
FORTUNE
NATIONAL Real Estate INVESTOR
Journal of Property Management
real estate today
BUILDING MANAGEMENT MAINTENANCE NEWS
ARCHITECTURAL RECORD
7

# Publications

Some real estate people eventually decide they want to do writing in the field. To write for a periodical on real estate, you must not only have a sound knowledge of the entire real estate industry and a nose for the new trends, but you also must have journalistic skills. A major in journalism is a good way to start, and courses in the numerous areas relating to the real estate industry are necessary.

Some of the real estate periodicals you can work for are listed in the chapter "For Further Information."

Most writers for magazines start off as researchers. This is not only excellent training in research, of course, but also in the organizing of material, which is one of the basic skills for a writer. Since real estate publications are limited in number, it is easier to gain experience in newspapers or magazines outside this area.

# Ethics

This is a sore point. How nice it would be if everybody in the world was as honest as the day is long, but alas, that is not the case. Although the various real estate organizations have done considerable work over the past twenty years or more to regulate the practice of real estate, there are still problems.

In his introduction to Anthony Wolff's book *Unreal Estate,* Stewart Udall asks with good reason why "ethical, *bona fide* developers and realtors, whose professions have been besmirched by these land speculators, have not led the fight to curb the excesses of this outlaw segment of their industry." He goes on to say that "The answer must lie in the fact that land speculation has deep roots in the American psyche. . . . Land greed has been a prominent trait in the American character from the beginning. . . . Gull-them-if-they're-gullible has been the common creed . . ."

We have talked to many honest brokers and salespeople, appraisers, managers and land speculators who regard their business as a profession that involves suiting both buyer and seller, landlord and tenant. And there are land developers who put an enormous amount of money, sweat, and time into planning developments and dividing them up in the best possible way. But there are developers who spend their time and money on lavish entertainment of prospective customers in order to sell them a piece of the desert with no water facilities, no roads, no anything—or perhaps a piece of land on the side of a hill too far from town for main sewage, and with soil too shallow to absorb sewage. There are those who sell lots in a swamp. Not only is this the worst place to build a house of any kind, but once built, the house becomes a cause of ecological damage as well.

The following story from the March 11, 1977, *New York Times* is relevant. It is a good example of one of the ways in which abuses come about.

The story was about four officials of the Amrep Corporation who had been sentenced to six months' imprisonment in connection with Rio Rancho Estates in New Mexico. Prospective investors—and most of them were *small* investors who could ill afford to lose money—were invited to free dinners to get them in the right frame of mind to pay an average of $11,800 per acre near Albuquerque. Rio Rancho was described by Amrep as a thriving community with 7,000 residents. The prosecutor said that Amrep knew that no more than 5 percent of the buyers would actually move to Rio Rancho. The *Times* went on to say: "Most of the investors had invested in Rio Rancho because of fraudulent promises that it was a safe investment that 'could double or triple their money in a few short years. There has been no resale market in Albuquerque for the land since Rio Rancho began more than 15 years ago,' Miss Hynes [the prosecutor] said, adding that 'These investors will never get their money back.'"

In the same issue, the *Times* reports that earlier in 1977, the McCulloch Oil Company "pleaded guilty to 19 misdemeanor counts of criminal fraud in connection with sales of its 27,000-acre Pueblo West subdivision in Colorado."

However it must be remembered that when a land speculator misbehaves, he or she is not acting alone. There are the county and state officials who have to approve a subdivision. Almost the worst aspect of land speculation is that government officials may not think about the consequences carefully enough before they give permission for a speculator to subdivide. They see that the county will benefit from the added taxes, but because the lots are unoccupied *for the time being,* officials think they will *never* have to provide the expensive services of police, schools, roads, etc. When lots are built on, then of course the homeowners need the usual services. So, combined greed and blundering can bring large populations into an area which simply is not equipped to deal with them. For example, in one Florida county, it was shown that every 1,000 new residents included 200 schoolchildren, 19 blind people, 67 old people, 11 juvenile delinquents, 16 alcoholics, and 30 mentally retarded children, all of whom needed specialized services. But of course it isn't the land developer who is going to take care of these needs; it is the taxpayers.

## DISCRIMINATION

The real estate industry could do a great deal more than it does now to prevent discrimination in housing on the grounds of race, creed, or national origin. The local realty board in a town could, if it chose to do so, crack down on real estate people who steer black and other minority buyers to certain areas and away from others. Every time a prejudiced homeowner puts his or her house up for sale, there is a real estate person involved who knows that a black purchaser will not be acceptable. And if the salesperson and broker only show the house to acceptable, i.e., white clients, they are violating the real estate code of ethics.

The President's Executive Order of 1962 meant that housing in any way connected to the federal government —whether through government mortgage loans, public housing, housing made possible by urban renewal projects, and housing owned by the federal government— came under an anti-discrimination mandate. This made it illegal to discriminate against a purchaser on the grounds of race, religion, color, national origin, or background. Then, in 1968, the open housing law prohibited racial discrimination by sellers and renters of buildings, homes, or apartments. A broker or salesperson who is involved in an act of discrimination (for example, telling a family a house has already been sold when it hasn't or inflating the price artificially to make it impossible for the family to buy) is in violation of the code of ethics of the National Association of Real Estate Boards and can lose his or her license.

# For Further Information

The realty board in your own town or city will be able to give you information about real estate and related courses offered at the state or two-year colleges in your area. They will also have details of adult education courses in real estate practice. All local boards are affiliated with the state and the NATIONAL ASSOCIATION OF REALTORS®.

**ORGANIZATIONS TO CONTACT**

**Appraisal Organizations**

*American Institute of Real Estate Appraisers*
430 North Michigan Avenue, Chicago, Illinois 60611.
This organization is affiliated with the National Association of Real Estate Boards. They issue a certificate of M.A.I., Member of Appraisal Institute, to those who have passed their stiff examinations.

*The American Society of Appraisers*
1028 Connecticut Avenue N.W., Washington, D.C. 20006.

*International Association of Assessing Officers*
1313 E. 60th Street, Chicago, Ill. 60637.

*Society of Real Estate Appraisers*
7 S. Dearborn Street, Chicago, Ill. 60603.
The Society has two classifications: Senior Real Estate Appraiser—commercial and industrial property—and Senior Residential Appraiser.

**Property Management**

*Institute of Real Estate Management*
430 North Michigan Avenue, Chicago, Illinois 60611.

*Apartment Owners and Managers Association of America*
65 Cherry Avenue, Watertown, Conn. 06795.

**Industrial Real Estate**

*American Industrial Real Estate Association*
5670 Wilshire Boulevard, Los Angeles, Calif. 90036.

*Commerce and Industry Association of New York, Inc.*
99 Church Street, New York, N.Y. 10007.

**Land Development**

*American Land Development Association*
1000 16th Street N.W., Washington, D.C. 20036.

**General**

*NATIONAL ASSOCIATION OF REALTORS®*
430 N. Michigan Avenue, Chicago, Ill. 60611.

*Canadian Real Estate Association*
99 Duncan Mill Road, Don Mills, Ontario.

**REAL ESTATE PUBLICATIONS**

This is a selected listing of some of the magazines published on real estate. Many of them are available on microfilm at your local library, and whatever your leanings may be in real estate, we suggest that you look at as many of them as you can to get an overall picture of what is going on in the industry today.

*A.I.R. Reports* (American Industrial Real Estate Assn.)
5670 Wilshire Boulevard, Los Angeles, Calif. 90036.

*American Land* (American Land Development Assn.)
1000 16th Street N.W., Washington, D.C. 20036.

*Apartment Owners News*
2868 E. Oakland Park Boulevard, Fort Lauderdale, Fla. 33306.

*Appraisal Journal* (American Institute of Real Estate Appraisers)
430 North Michigan Avenue, Chicago, Ill. 60611.

*Building and Realty Record*
121 Chestnut Street, Philadelphia, Penn. 19106.

*Condominium World*
89 Beach Street, Boston, Mass. 02111.

*International Assessor*
1313 E. 60th Street, Chicago, Ill. 60637.

*Mortgage and Real Estate Executives Report*
89 Beach Street, Boston, Mass. 02111.

*Real Estate Appraiser*
7 S. Dearborn Street, Chicago, Ill. 60603.

*Real Estate Investment Planning*
I.B.P. Plaza, Englewood Cliffs, N.J. 07632.

*Real Estate Investor*
306 Dartmouth Street, Boston, Mass. 02116.

*Real Estate Review*
89 Beach Street, Boston, Mass. 02111.

*Real Estate Today*
430 North Michigan Avenue, Chicago, Ill. 60611.

*Realty*
156 E. 52nd Street, New York, N.Y. 10022.

# For Further Reading

There are a large number of books on real estate, and we are listing just a few of them here to start you off. The ones listed below are written in plain language and give a good overall picture of some of the problems and situations you are likely to come up against.

Case, Frederick E. *Real Estate Brokerage.* Englewood Cliffs, N.J.: Prentice-Hall, 1965.

Gross, Jerome. *Concise Desk Guide to Real Estate Practice.* Englewood Cliffs, N.J.: Prentice-Hall, 1976.

────── *Illustrated Encyclopaedic Dictionary of Real Estate Terms.* Englewood Cliffs, N.J.: Prentice-Hall, 1969.

Semenow, Robert W. *Questions and Answers on Real Estate.* 7th ed. Englewood Cliffs, N.J.: Prentice-Hall, 1972.

# Index

Accounting, 6, 46
Activities, 23, 28
Advertising, 28, 35
Age, 22–23
Aggression, 22
Agricultural land, 45
Apartments, 2, 27, 41, 42, 44, 54, 60
Appearance, 22, 23, 31
Appraisal, 45–49, 52
Architecture, 8, 11, 17, 33, 46
Attitude, 22
Automobiles, 23

Balance sheet, 51
Bankruptcy, 17
Banks, 17, 34, 50
Blueprints, 34–35
Bonds, 32
Bookkeeping, 6
Brokers
    commercial, 11–12, 20
    competition between, 15, 42
    duties of, 4–11
    failures of, 17
    industrial, 13–14
    land, 12–13
    offices of, 14
    residential, 20, 33
    training of, 4–5, 6
Building codes, 3
Buses, 53
Business
    administration, 6, 15, 17, 46, 52
    management, 4, 17
    small, 4–11, 14–17

Canadian Real Estate Association, 18, 46, 54

Case, Frederick E., 21, 27–28
Civil service examinations, 54
Clients, former, 27
Code of ethics, 31
College, 4, 17, 22, 25–26, 44, 46, 54, 57
Commercial
    broker, 11–12, 20
    district, 14
    selling, 26–27, 34
Commissions, 5, 8, 15, 18–20, 21, 23, 37
Communities, 8–11, 28, 33, 35
Competition, 15, 42
Condominiums, 2, 34
*Concise Desk Guide to Real Estate Practice and Procedure* (Gross), 50
Construction industry, 3, 11, 32–33
Contractors, 32–33
Cooperatives, 2
Corporations, 38–41
Correspondence courses, 17
Counseling, 51–52
Courts, 53

Day care centers, 52
Deeds, 31–32
Degrees, 17, 46, 50, 52
Developers, 33
Discrimination, 60
Doctoral degree, 50
Documents, 31–32
Door-to-door soliciting, 28
Drop-in trade, 14, 28

Ecology, 58
Economics, 4, 17, 34, 52
Economy, 3, 6, 33, 42

[64]

Education, 17–18, 52
Engineers, 8, 11, 33, 46
Equity investment, 49
Estimates, 3, 32
Ethics, 57–60
Examinations, 18, 46, 54
Experience, personal, 25
Experience, previous, 22, 52

Factories, 13–14, 33, 34
Failures, in brokerage, 17
File clerk, 18
Finance, 17
Financial status, 23
"For Sale by Owner" signs, 28
Foreclosures, 54

Government, 8, 11, 50
    real estate service, 52–54
Graduate work, 17
Gross, Jerome, 50

Health services, 53
High school, 17, 18, 22
Highway construction contractors, 33
Highways, 33
Honesty, 22, 57–60
Hospitals, 53
Hotels, 42
Houses, 2, 21, 25–26, 27, 33

Industrial
    broker, 13–14
    selling, 26–27
Inflation, 41, 49, 50
Inspections, 38
Institute for Real Estate Management, 44, 45
Insurance companies, 5, 23, 34, 50
    and property management, 35–38
Interviews, 21–23
Investment, 49, 53, 58–59
    counseling, 51–52
    on the job, 50–51
    protective committees, 34

Journalism, 57
Judgement, 22

Labor
    relations, 42–44
    unions, 35
Land
    agricultural, 45
    broker, 12–13
    speculation, 57–60
Law, 17, 46
    affecting real estate, 3, 6
    zoning, 3, 6, 13, 35, 46, 49
Lease, 2, 4, 38–41
Libraries, 52
License, 4, 5, 6, 20
    requirements, 17–18
Listings. *See* Multiple-listing system
Loans, 31, 32
Location, 45

Mail, direct, 28
Maintenance, 51
Management. *See* Property management
Management companies, 38
Manners, 22, 31
Maps, 31
Marital status, 23
Mass transit, 33
Master's degree, 46, 50
Media, 6, 28, 35
Military installations, 42
Mobile homes, 2, 42
Mortgage, 50, 60
    deed, 32
Multiple-listing system, 15, 27–28, 31
Museums, 53

National Association of Real Estate Boards, 4, 46, 60

[65]

National Association of Realtors, 17, 18
Neighborhoods, 6, 21, 26, 31, 32, 33, 35, 45, 46
New York City, 52
*New York Times,* 58–59
Newspapers, 28, 57

Office, 2, 11–12, 14, 38, 42
    jobs, 18, 22

Personality, 21
Plumbing, 41
Police stations, 53
Policy book, 31
Pollution, 14
Prisons, 52
Property, defects in, 25
Property management, 34–45
    and insurance companies, 35–38
    and management companies, 38
Property values, constant change in, 3, 5–6, 35
Prospect file, 31
Psychology, 17, 35
Public housing, 54, 60
Public relations activities, 28
Publications, 57

Real estate
    changing property values, 3, 5–6, 35
    dishonesty in, 57–60
    government service, 52–54
    investment counseling, 51–52
    laws affecting, 3, 6
    women in, 25
*Real Estate Brokerage* (Case), 21
Realty board, 15, 18, 60
Record-keeping, 17
References, 22
Remodeling, 32
Rental agent, 18

Residential
    broker, 20, 33
    selling, 20, 25–26, 33

Salaries, 18, 20, 21, 44, 46, 52
Sales, 20–33
    commercial, 26–27, 34
    goals, 15
    industrial, 26–27
    residential, 20, 25–26, 33
Salesperson, 18, 20
    on the job, 27–33
    selling abilities, 20–23
Sanitation department, 53
Schools, 52
Sewage, 13, 58
Slums, 3
Sociology, 46
Speaking ability, 21
Stock market crash, 34
Street construction contractors, 33
Subways, 53

Tax offices, 53
Taxes, 3, 13, 49, 51, 54, 59
Title insurance, 32
Trust companies, 34

Udall, Stewart, 58
University of Wisconsin, 46
*Unreal Estate* (Wolff), 58
Urban renewal projects, 60

Vacation homes, 12–13, 33

Warehouses, 14
Water supply, 13, 26–27
Wolff, Anthony, 58
Women, in real estate, 25
Work habits, 31

Zoning laws, 3, 6, 13, 35, 46, 49